A SIGNATURE IN TIME

CONTEMPORARY SAMPLERS TO STITCH

By The Vanessa-Ann Collection

Sedgewood® Press

New York

ACKNOWLEDGMENTS

For Sedgewood® Press

Elizabeth P. Rice, Director
Leslie Gilbert, Associate Editor
Bill Rose, Production Manager

For The Vanessa-Ann Collection®—

Terrece Beesley Woodruff, Owner, Designer
Jo Packham Buehler, Owner, Designer
Margaret Shields Marti, Executive Editor, Designer
Heather Hales, Editor
Monica Smith, Editor
Trice Liljenquist Boerens, Art Director, Designer
Nancy Whitley, Needlework Director
Julie Truman, Layout, Designer
Susan Jorgensen, Graphing
Pamela Randall, Operations Director
Barbara Milburn, Administrative Assistant
Annette Morris, Customer Relations

Additional Designs by:
Barbara Heward
Liz Mueller
Tina Richards

Trice Liljenquist Boerens, Illustrations
Holly Fuller, Calligraphy
Ryne Hazen, Photography

First printing: 1987
Library of Congress number: 85-63721
ISBN: 0-02-496790-4

Published by Sedgewood® Press

Distributed by Macmillan Publishing Company, a division
of Macmillan, Inc.

To Nancy and our stitchers~

You have sewn together
    with threads of gold
A sampler of memories
    for us to hold.

Each stitch you took
    with loving care
To help us remember
    The moments shared.

And somewhere in time,
    when these we see,
We shall always hear,
    "Remember me."

From a place in our heart
    so secret and small
For your "Signature In Time"
    we thank you all.

TABLE OF CONTENTS

My love affair with samplers is an old one. Its beginnings fuse with my appreciation for fine china and quality wood furniture. It may never, however, know greater fervor than it did on a comfortable spring morning in May of 1984. My friend and I were concluding a stay in New York City and had begun the morning combining business and personal interests along Madison Avenue. When we found ourselves about a block from the Smithsonian's Cooper-Hewitt Museum, we approached it with casual interest, and that mostly for the building itself.

Happening upon some one hundred samplers in the rooms of the museum's second floor stirred an array of emotions! My pulse raced as I inspected those ancient fabrics, spun and woven by hand, which are now fragile, gray and sometimes damaged. None of the colors were ever bright and most, by now, had faded into lovely, soft tones that only suggest what they had once been. The verses on the pieces were hopes and prayers composed in Latin, Spanish, French, and English. Their origins were the hands of women over a span of 1250 years.

Degas and Manet I enjoy. Frank Lloyd Wright I study. But it is the artists of the samplers for whom I have an understanding and with whom I have a deep, common bond. These designs are from the hearts of women with little or no training in art or literature, who may have spun and woven the fabric in their sampler. I find myself imagining the story behind each stitcher and sampler. In my mind, they become proud or humble, rich and stylish or immigrants seeking fame and fortune. Most of them were ordinary. Many were young and worked their samplers under the direction of a relative or teacher. They probably had interests similar to and attention spans much like my own children. The adults whose work I enjoy must have had days filled with joys and anxieties. I hope their hours with their needlework served as a tonic for frayed nerves, just as mine does for me.

Today's samplers are being designed by women who appreciate the same values. They, too, are making a very personal statement and are using their skills to commemorate a feeling or an occasion. These women no longer embroider a monogram on their linens but they apply as much care and attention to their stitches and colors. Their completed work is displayed with equal pride and importance.

Every sampler ever stitched, regardless of the design, stitcher's age or heritage, the colors or the size, is a way of leaving one's mark in a small way, a way of saying "remember me," and a way of providing a touch of beauty and warmth.

Someday I shall design and stitch my own sampler. It is likely to be cross-stitched in dark reds, greens and blues on a cream background. A saying would need to be especially meaningful. It will probably reflect my interests in my family and nature. It will read "Margaret Shields Marti" and, perhaps, "Age 80."

M.S.M.
1986

SAMPLERS: A SIGNATURE IN TIME

A sampler — meaning nearly any "sample" of needlework — is a personal reflection; every sampler reveals something about the stitcher and her milieu. The earliest European samplers date from the sixteenth century, though the pieces most familiar to connoisseurs are later works from colonial America and the Victorian age in Europe. Needlework itself is thousands of years old, however, with one early example discovered on clothing in a Siberian burial chamber from the fifth and fourth centuries b.c. From any era, a sampler is an individual work of art — and each one is different, even those from the same classroom of girls or from the same embroiderer at different times in her life.

Today samplers are prized collector's items as examples of an American collectible made by children. A large alphabet sampler with a colorful border in good condition is most valued, and the rarest piece is the miniature, a work that may be less than five inches square. An undated anonymous sampler with only a simple alphabet is sought least by collectors.

Long before they became collector's items samplers were simply pieces of cloth on which needleworkers practiced embroidery and mending techniques. For generations samplers were catalogs of stitches serving as "how to" books for women in households. In sixteenth century Europe samplers were the work of the elite: nuns, women in the courts, and women of wealth. In America, especially during the 1700s, they were a standard part of the curriculum for schoolgirls, some of whom began their stitching at the young age of six. The prevailing attitude of the era was that embroidery was an indispensable accomplishment, though not every girl who made a sampler was happy to do so; one Patty Polk, a ten-year-old from Kent County, Maryland, left a record of her feelings in no uncertain terms. Her sampler, from about 1800, reads: "Patty Polk did this and she hated every stitch she did in it. She loves to read much more."

While no specific characteristics define a piece as a sampler, the combination of several features identify this genre: the alphabet, a maxim, Bible verse, or poem, geometric designs and a decorative border, the date, initials or a name may be combined with artwork in an unlimited number of ways. During the time that samplers were considered a learning exercise or reference, the pieces were stored. Later, as samplers came to be considered works of art in themselves, they were framed — as most are today — and hung on home and museum walls.

Sampler styles generally fall into four categories: pictorial; family record; alphabet/verse; and map. A pictorial sampler might have been a rendition of a house, people and animals, a Biblical scene or a collection of motifs such as hearts, plants, and public buildings. Sometimes overlooked is the mourning or memorial sampler, which was popular in the 1800s and often pictured a monument, weeping relatives, weeping trees, and water. Family record samplers included the names of family members, sometimes recording dates of births and deaths, perhaps in the format of a family tree.

The alphabet/verse sampler, often with numerals, was used to teach the basics of spelling and sewing, particularly to young students. It was common to add a poem, saying, or Bible verse, some of which were moralistic and quite lengthy. Alphabet samplers were expected to be used later as patterns for monograms on household linens and lingerie. It is interesting to note that certain letters of the alphabet were routinely omitted. One explanation is that in some local European communities the alphabet did not include the letters Y and Z. Often U and V were deleted because W could serve as a stitching model for both; X, Y, and Z may have been left out because they are letters just not used very much. The simple matter of lack of space may have also dictated the omission of a letter or two. Map samplers, which are least seldom copied today, were also used as teaching tools for geography, spelling, and embroidery.

The stitcher almost always included her name and age at the time she did the work, though she might try to conceal the facts later. One eighteenth-century sampler reveals that Mary Hafline made it in her eleventh year. The date, however, reads "178," with the omission of the fourth digit indicating she did not want her age calculated. Another woman anxious to destroy the evidence of her age left a neatly cut-out space where her name and the date should have been.

Even those samplers without names or dates often yield clues to their origin through characteristics that can be identified with a particular geographic region or a style peculiar to a specific period of time. A Dutch sampler, for example, probably would have included the coat of arms or the traditional symbol of the city in which the stitcher lived: a pair of rabbits represented Amsterdam while one rabbit represented Middelburg. Samplers from countries that were predominantly Roman Catholic, such as Italy, always introduced the alphabet with a cross and may have included a number of other religious motifs. German samplers varied with the region and were often somber-looking pieces embroidered in black with circular or floral motifs or religious symbols. Verses were unusual in these German works.

Scandinavian samplers were sedate and restrained with sparse stitchery on small pieces of fabric. French samplers made during the nineteenth century used cross-stitch in a peculiarly French way, with one passage of the needle across the cloth in a looping backward movement. Characteristically, nineteenth-century Italian samplers had unhemmed edges with no precaution taken against fraying, while those from northern Europe often displayed carefully worked decorative hemstitching.

American samplers reflected patterns of immigration. A stitched piece from Massachusetts was likely to resemble an English sampler; Pennsylvanian works had German motifs. Those made by schoolchildren often reflected the country of the teacher's origin. The family record sampler and pieces with black backgrounds, which were solid areas of either cross-stitch or long and floating backstitches, are unique to American samplers.

Even the shape or fabric of a sampler can reflect its origin. The earliest American works, from the seventeenth century, were long and narrow like their English counterparts. At that time special fabrics were manufactured in Britain and northern Europe to be used as foundation fabrics for needlework. Nearly always a plain-weave linen cotton or wool, these fabrics were woven on narrow looms that produced a piece twelve to fifteen inches wide with blue threads at the selvage edges. Sometimes these narrow strips were stitched together. Sampler shapes had broadened and were less restricted in composition by the mid-eighteenth century. Around the nineteenth century they became nearly square, allowing additional space for verses and decorative illustrations.

Some designs were worked in silk threads brought to America from the Orient through Europe. Occasionally a community in the United States, most often in the Deep South, would experiment in silk culture. Mormons who settled Utah in the mid-1800s tried producing their own silk. One record from a pioneer child's diary reads: "Aunt Nancy reeled the silk from some of the cocoons and dyed the skeins which we used for our artwork. These we put in suitable frames, so for years the Lord's Prayer, the Ten Commandments, and 'God Bless Our Home' were ever before us."

For the most part the colors used in early samplers were soft and simple shades of blue, green, yellow, rose, red, gold, and brown. One needlework historian described the result as "soft, delicate, tapestry-like colors and exquisitely fine cross-stitch on yellow, mellow old linen or canvas."

Today samplers are stitched by women from all walks of life, providing a source of satisfaction and decoration much as they have for generations. Artists are creating needlework designs that reflect — as samplers have always done — contemporary tastes, styles, and technology. Traditional characteristics of early samplers (border styles, alphabets, and the inclusion of a saying or poem, for example) are often carried over to today's designs. And some women are stitching replicas of bygone days, copied from museum or privately held antique pieces.

Most contemporary sampler designs are published in charts that are printed in books and leaflets readily available to needleworkers. The most popular are worked in counted cross-stitch (a movement that had been popular in western Europe for some time and swept across America, beginning in the Deep South, during the second half of the twentieth century). But patterns for other needlework techniques, such as embroidery, candlewicking, or filet, are also available. the individuality of today's samplers will surely be of historical interest to needleworkers of the future.

BIBLIOGRAPHY

Boone, Gray. "Antique samplers enrich America's folk heritage." Birmingham *News* (January, 1986).

Brown, Georgiana. *American Needlework.* New York: Harbeson-Coward-McCain, 1938.

Embroidered Samplers in the Collection of the Cooper-Hewitt Museum. New York: The Smithsonian Institution, 1984.

Grunwald, H.A., ed. *The Encyclopedia of Collectibles.* Alexandria, Va.: Time-Life Books. Pages 88-99.

Krueger, Glee F. *A Gallery of American Samplers; the Theodore H. Kapnek Collection.* New York: E.P. Dutton, 1978.

Paxman, Shirley B. *Domestic Arts and Crafts of Mormon Pioneers.* Salt Lake City, Utah: Deseret Book Company, 1976.

Ring, Betty. *Let Virtue Be a Guide to Thee; Needlework in the Education of Rhode Island Women, 1730-1830.* Providence, R.I.: The Rhode Historical Society, 1983.

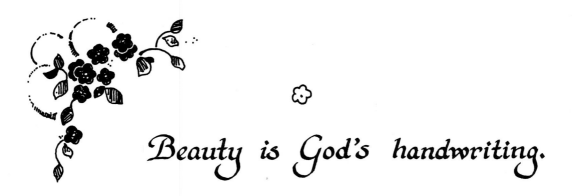

Beauty is God's handwriting.

—Charles Kingsley——————

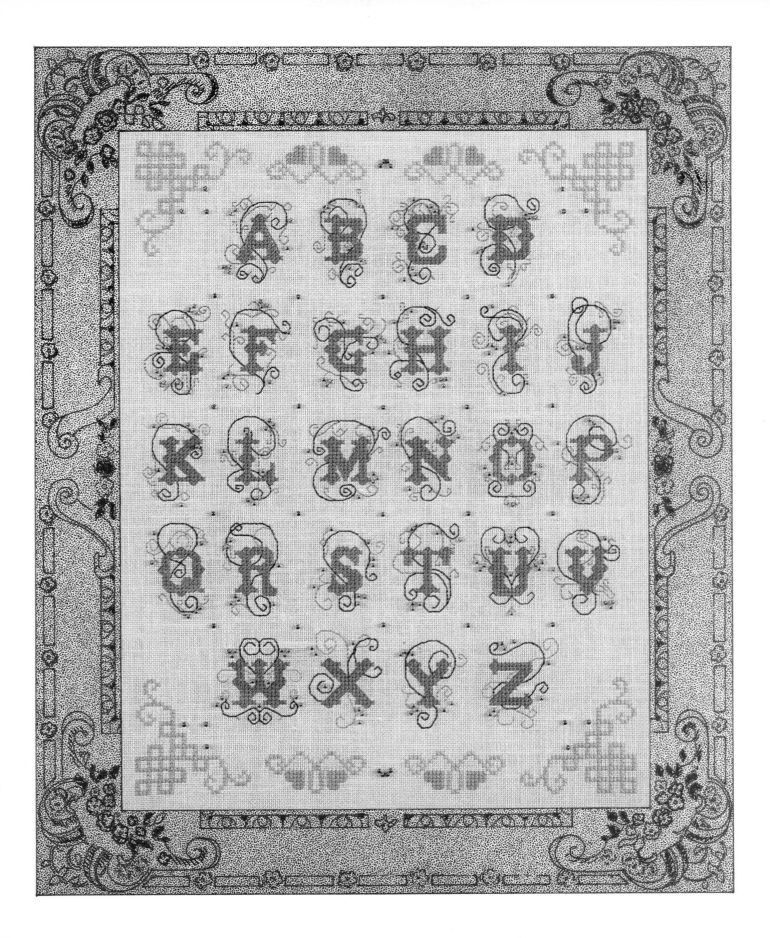

Stitch Count

A VICTORIAN ALPHABET

Cover Sample: Stitched on Cream Belfast Linen 32 over two threads. Finished design size is 8⅛″ × 10⅝″. Cut fabric 14″ × 17″. Finished design sizes using other fabrics are: Aida 11 – 11⅞″ × 15½″; Aida 14 – 9¼″ × 12¼″; Aida 18 – 7¼″ × 9½″; Hardanger 22 – 5⅞″ × 7¾″.

Bates		DMC (used for cover sample)	
		Step One: Cross-stitch (two strands)	
887	•	3046	Yellow Beige - med.
893	✕ ⊠	224	Shell Pink - lt.
894	⋅ ⊿	223	Shell Pink - med.
		Step Two: Back Stitch (one strand)	
875		503	Blue Green - med.
878		501	Blue Green - dk.
		Step Three: Bead Work	
	△	Rose	
	•	Ice Green	

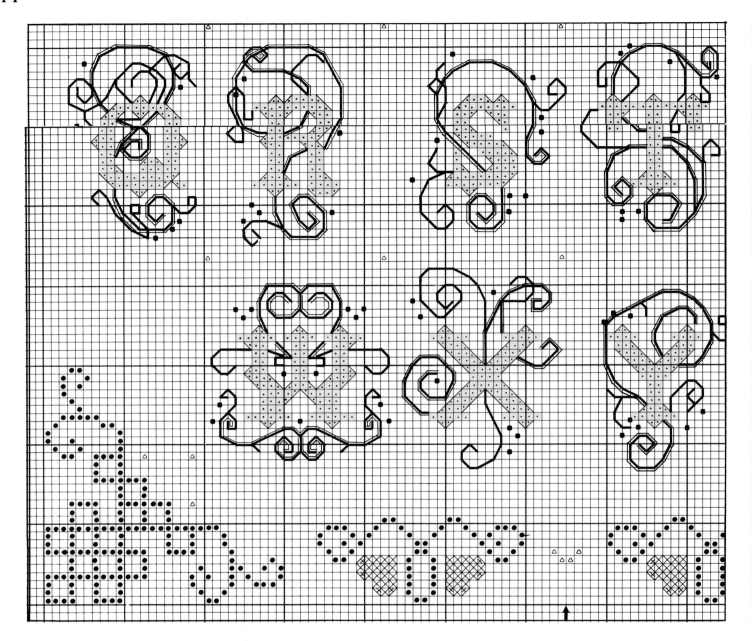

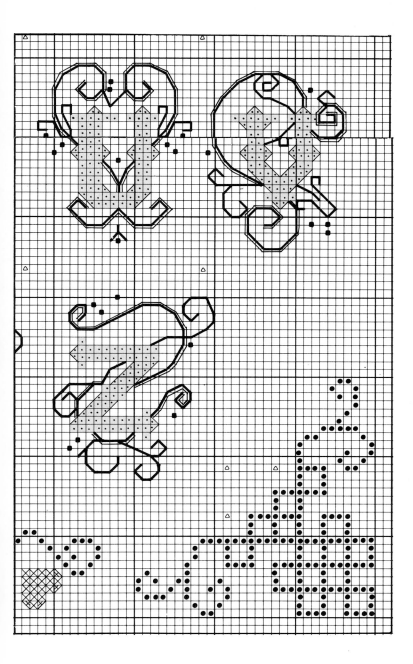

A VICTORIAN ALPHABET

Cover Sample: Stitched on Cream Belfast Linen 32 over two threads. Finished design size is 8⅛″ × 10⅝″. Cut fabric 14″ × 17″. Finished design sizes using other fabrics are: Aida 11 – 11⅞″ × 15½″; Aida 14 – 9¼″ × 12¼″; Aida 18 – 7¼″ × 9½″; Hardanger 22 – 5⅞″ × 7¾″.

Bates		DMC (used for cover sample)	
		Step One: Cross-stitch (two strands)	
887	●	3046	Yellow Beige - med.
893	✕	224	Shell Pink - lt.
894	•	223	Shell Pink - med.
		Step Two: Back Stitch (one strand)	
875		503	Blue Green - med.
878		501	Blue Green - dk.
		Step Three: Bead Work	
	△	Rose	
	●	Ice Green	

16

When this you see, remember me,
And bear me in your mind.
What others say when I'm away,
Speak of me as you find.

—Old Sampler Verse—

The antique sampler from which this design was patterned is owned by Suzanne Sarver of Ogden, Utah. She purchased the piece in 1974 from an antique dealer in Michigan.

To personalize graph, refer to alphabet on page 163.

Stitch Count

205

193

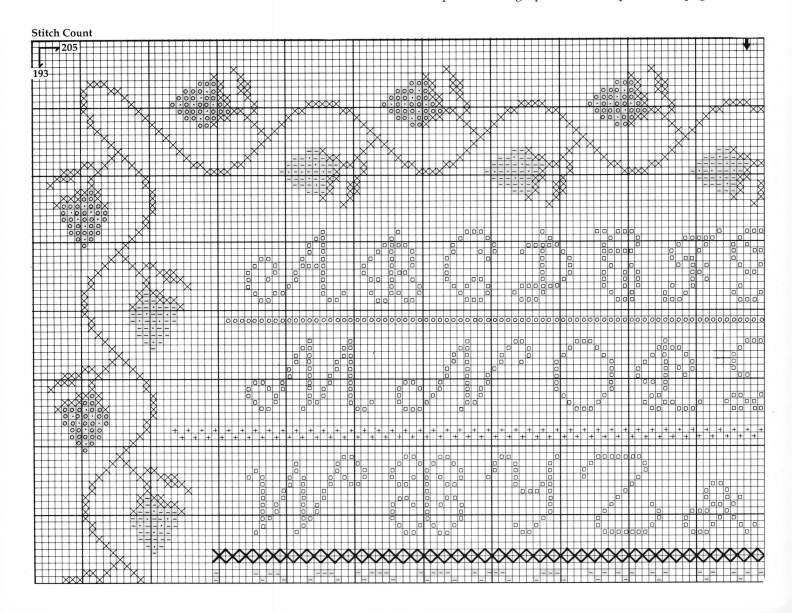

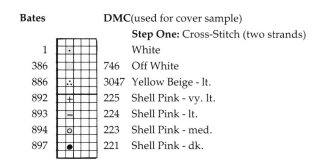

FROM THE PAST ✗

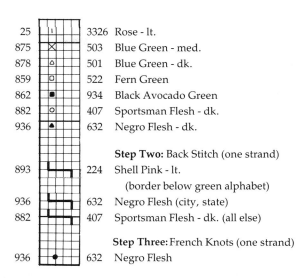

Cover Sample: Stitched on Cream Belfast Linen 32 over two threads. Finished design size is 12 ¾″ × 12″. Cut fabric 19″ × 18″. Finished design sizes using other fabrics are: Aida 11 – 18⅝″ × 17⅝″; Aida 14 – 14⅝″ × 13¾″; Aida 18 – 11⅜″ × 10¾″; Hardanger 22 – 9¼″ × 8¾″.

Bates		DMC	(used for cover sample)
		Step One:	Cross-Stitch (two strands)
1	·		White
386		746	Off White
886	∴	3047	Yellow Beige - lt.
892	+	225	Shell Pink - vy. lt.
893	−	224	Shell Pink - lt.
894	o	223	Shell Pink - med.
897	●	221	Shell Pink - dk.

25	I	3326	Rose - lt.
875	✗	503	Blue Green - med.
878	△	501	Blue Green - dk.
859	▢	522	Fern Green
862	■	934	Black Avocado Green
882	o	407	Sportsman Flesh - dk.
936	▲	632	Negro Flesh - dk.

Step Two: Back Stitch (one strand)

893		224	Shell Pink - lt.
			(border below green alphabet)
936		632	Negro Flesh (city, state)
882		407	Sportsman Flesh - dk. (all else)

Step Three: French Knots (one strand)

936	●	632	Negro Flesh

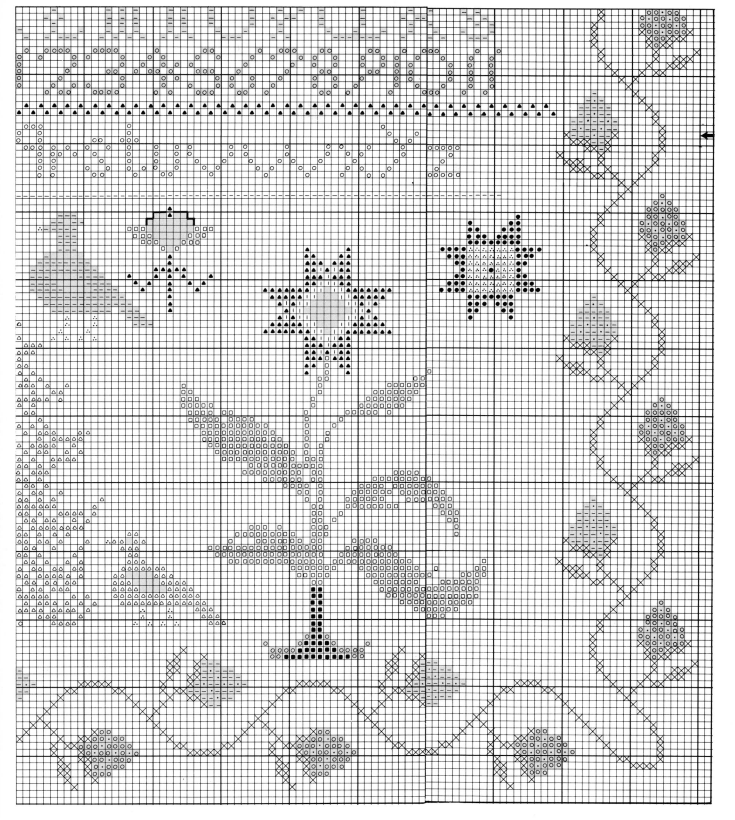

A day in the country
is worth a month in town.

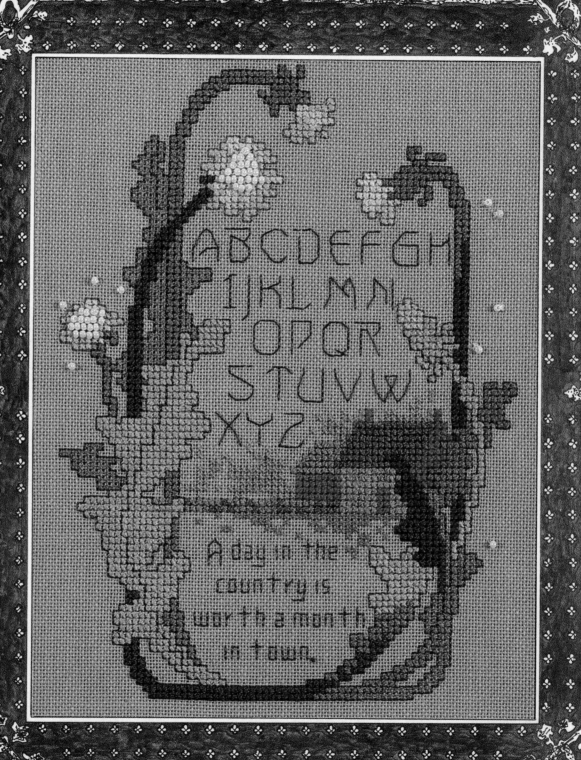

A DAY IN THE COUNTRY

Cover Sample: Stitched on Khaki Linda 27 over two threads. Finished design size is 5⅜" × 7⅛". Cut fabric 12" × 13". Finished design sizes using other fabrics are: Aida 11 – 6⅝" × 8¾"; Aida 14 – 5¼" × 6⅞"; Aida 18 – 4" × 5⅜"; Hardanger 22 – 3⅜" × 4⅜".

Bates		DMC	(used for cover sample
		Step One:	Cross-stitch (three strands)
842	·	3013	Khaki Green - lt.
859	▽	3052	Gray Green - med.
846	⊠	3051	Gray Green - dk.
886	=	3047	Yellow Beige - lt.
887	▫	3046	Yellow Beige - med.
363	·	436	Tan
370	●	434	Brown - lt.
900	○	647	Beaver Gray - med.
8581	⊠	646	Beaver Gray - dk.
		Step Two:	Filet Cross-stitch (one strand)
849	∴	927	Slate Green - med.
859	I	3052	Gray Green - med.
		Step Three:	Back Stitch (one strand)
370		434	Brown - lt. (flowers)
846		3051	Gray Green - dk. (all else)
		Step Four:	French Knots (one strand)
846	●	3051	Gray Green - dk.
		Step Five:	Bead Work
	▲		Cream

Stitch Count

A day in the
country is
worth a month
in town.

You never really leave a place you love...
Part of it you take with you,
leaving a part of you behind.

—Anonymous—

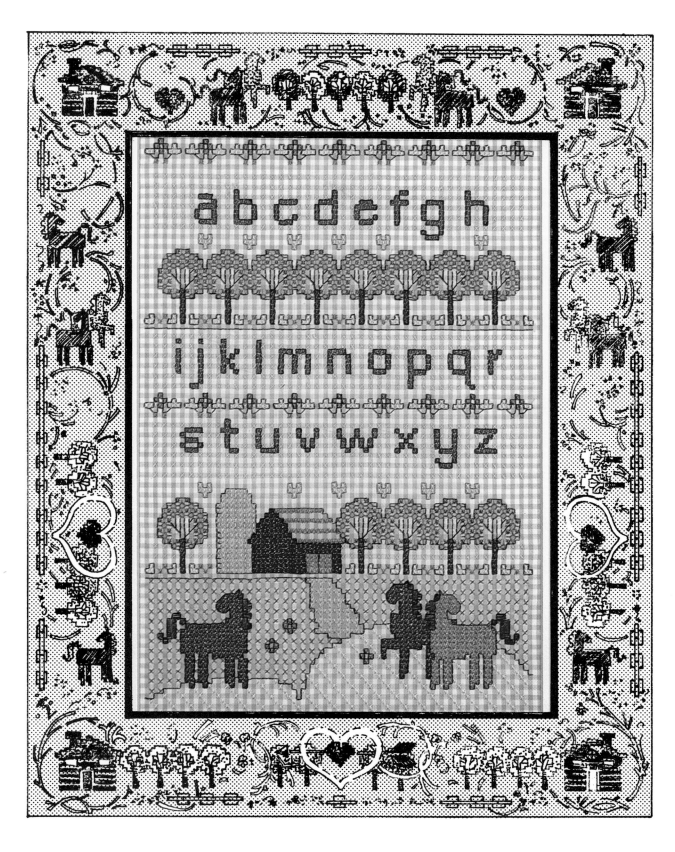

Stitch Count

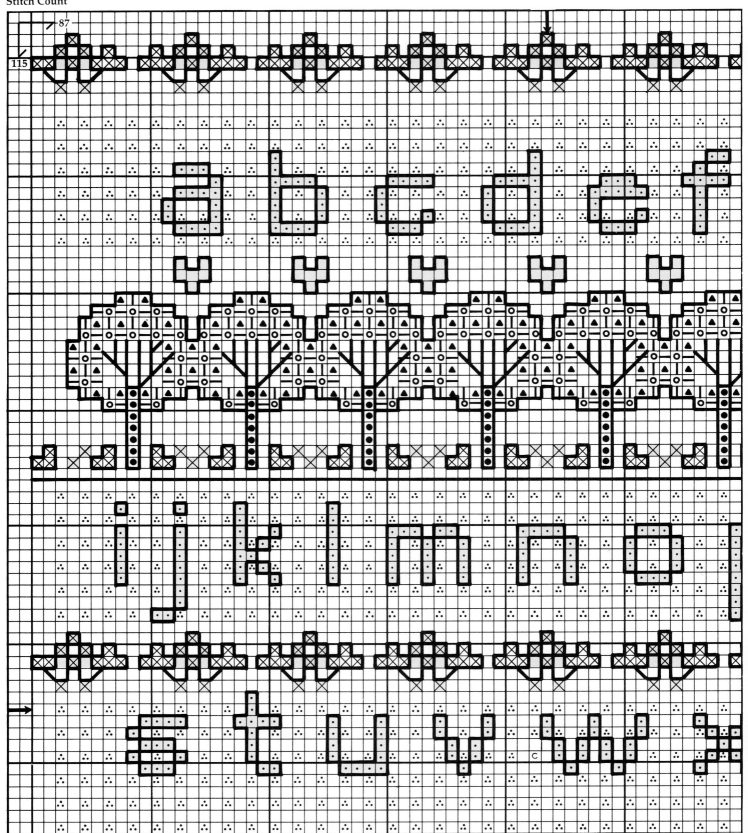

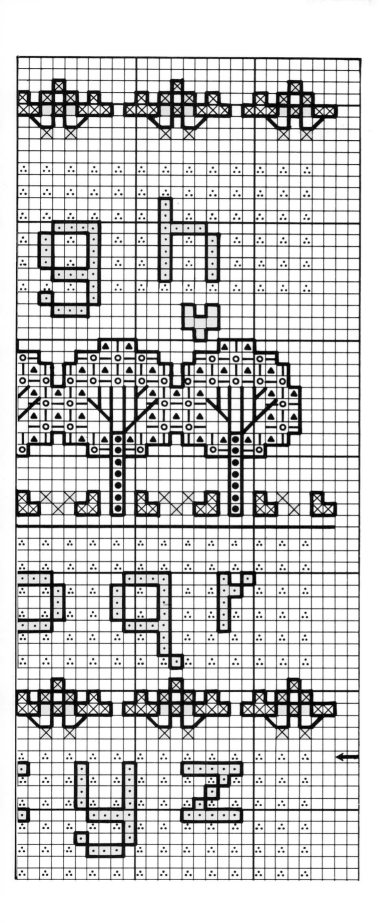

Cover Sample for Chicken-scratch: Stitched on ⅛″ lavender gingham fabric. Finished design size is 11⅜″ × 15⅞″. Cut fabric 20″ × 24″; see Step 1 of Chicken-scratch Instructions, page 163.

Cover Sample for Cross-stitch: Stitched on Cream Hardanger 22 over two threads. Finished design size is 7⅞″ × 10½″. Cut fabric 14″ × 17″. Finished design sizes using other fabrics are: Aida 11 – 7⅞″ × 10½″; Aida 14 – 6¼″ × 8¼″; Aida 18 – 4⅞″ × 6⅜″; Hardanger 22 – 4″ × 5¼″.

Bates		DMC (used for cover sample)	
		Step One: Cross-stitch over dark square of fabric (two strands)	
968	c	778	Antique Mauve - lt.
		Step Two: Smyrna-cross (two strands) /optional cross-stitch (two strands)	
968		778	Antique Mauve - lt.
69	·	3687	Mauve
70	▪	3685	Mauve - dk.
118	✗	340	Blue Violet - med.
206	✗	955	Nile Green - lt.
210	▲	562	Jade - med.
914	– /	3064	Sportsman Flesh - med.
936	● ◢	632	Negro Flesh
398	·	415	Pearl Gray
		Step Three: Woven Stitch (two strands) /optional cross-stitch (two strands)	
210	⊖	562	Jade - med.
		Step Four: Cross-stitch (two strands)	
968	∴	778	Antique Mauve - lt.
210	⊡	562	Jade - med.
		Step Five: Loose Stitch (two strands)	
936	‖‖	632	Negro Flesh
		Step Six: Back Stitch (one strand)	
69		3687	Mauve (hearts)
879		500	Blue Green - vy. dk. (tree tops)
381		938	Coffee Brown - ultra dk. (all else)

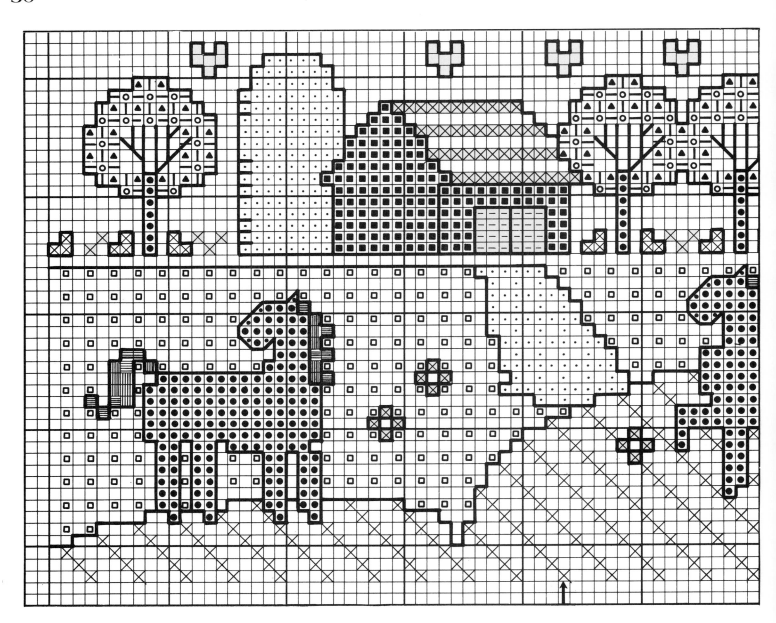

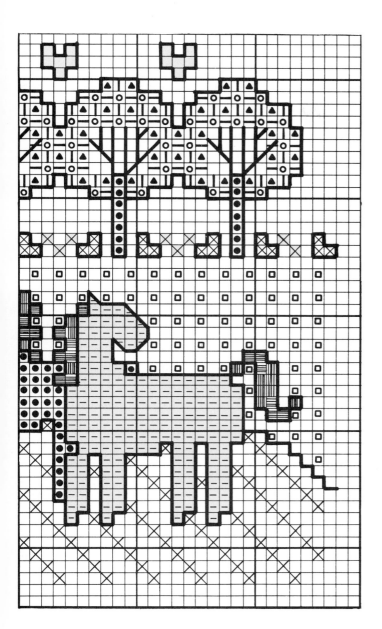

THE HOME PLACE

Cover Sample for Chicken-scratch: Stitched on ⅛" lavender gingham fabric. Finished design size is 11⅜" × 15⅞". Cut fabric 20" × 24"; see Step 1 of Chicken-scratch Instructions, page 163.

Cover Sample for Cross-stitch: Stitched on Cream Hardanger 22 over two threads. Finished design size is 7⅞" × 10½". Cut fabric 14" × 17". Finished design sizes using other fabrics are: Aida 11 – 7⅞" × 10½"; Aida 14 – 6¼" × 8¼"; Aida 18 – 4⅞" × 6⅜"; Hardanger 22 – 4" × 5¼".

Bates		DMC	(used for cover sample)
			Step One: Cross-stitch over dark square of fabric (two strands)
968	c	778	Antique Mauve - lt.
			Step Two: Smyrna-cross (two strands) /optional cross-stitch (two strands)
968		778	Antique Mauve - lt.
69	·	3687	Mauve
70	∎	3685	Mauve - dk.
118	✕	340	Blue Violet - med.
206	✕	955	Nile Green - lt.
210	▲	562	Jade - med.
914	−	3064	Sportsman Flesh - med.
936	● ◢	632	Negro Flesh
398	·	415	Pearl Gray
			Step Three: Woven Stitch (two strands) /optional cross-stitch (two strands)
210		562	Jade - med.
			Step Four: Cross-stitch (two strands)
968	∴	778	Antique Mauve - lt.
210	▫	562	Jade - med.
			Step Five: Loose Stitch (two strands)
936	‖‖‖	632	Negro Flesh
			Step Six: Back Stitch (one strand)
69		3687	Mauve (hearts)
879		500	Blue Green - vy. dk. (tree tops)
381		938	Coffee Brown - ultra dk. (all else)

Friendship is the golden thread...

ABCDEFGHI
JKLMNOPQR
STUVWXYZ

FRIENDSHIP IS
THE GOLDEN THREAD
THAT TIES THE HEARTS
OF ALL THE WORLD

KDT   1985

A SAMPLER FOR A FRIEND

Cover Sample: Stitched on White Belfast Linen 32 over two threads. Finished design size is 3¾″ × 8¾″. Cut fabric 10″ × 15″. Finished design sizes using other fabrics are: Aida 11 – 5½″ × 12⅞″; Aida 14 – 4⅜″ × 10″; Aida 18 – 3⅜″ × 7¾″; Hardanger 22 – 2¾″ × 6⅜″.

Bates		DMC (used for cover sample)
		Step One: Cross-stitch (two strands)
881		945 Sportsman Flesh
969		316 Antique Mauve - med.
970		315 Antique Mauve - dk.

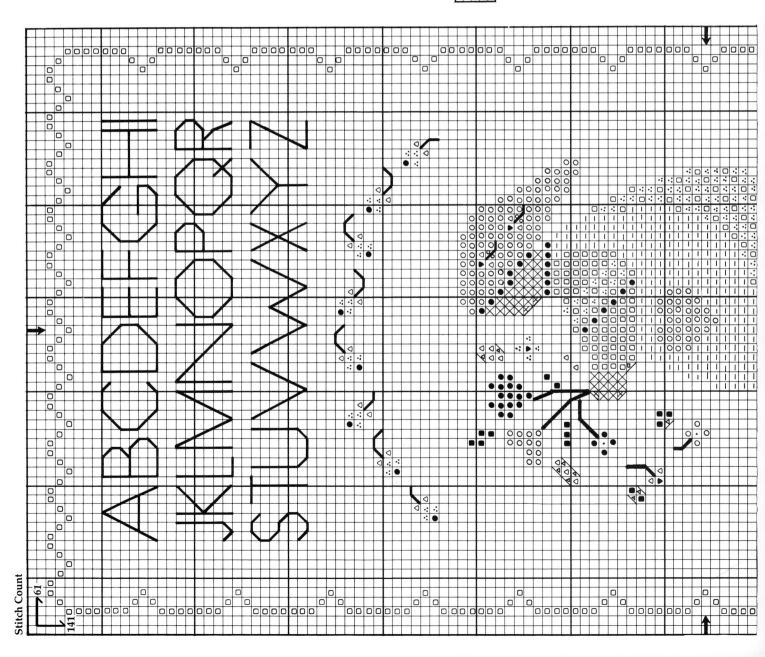

Stitch Count
61
141

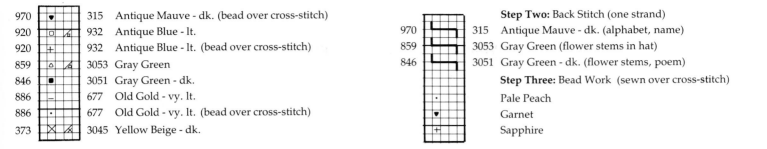

970	▼	315	Antique Mauve - dk. (bead over cross-stitch)
920	□ ⬙	932	Antique Blue - lt.
920	+	932	Antique Blue - lt. (bead over cross-stitch)
859	△ ◪	3053	Gray Green
846	●	3051	Gray Green - dk.
886	–	677	Old Gold - vy. lt.
886	·	677	Old Gold - vy. lt. (bead over cross-stitch)
373	✕ ◪	3045	Yellow Beige - dk.

Step Two: Back Stitch (one strand)

970		315	Antique Mauve - dk. (alphabet, name)
859		3053	Gray Green (flower stems in hat)
846		3051	Gray Green - dk. (flower stems, poem)

Step Three: Bead Work (sewn over cross-stitch)

·	Pale Peach
▼	Garnet
+	Sapphire

To personalize graph, refer to alphabet on page 162.

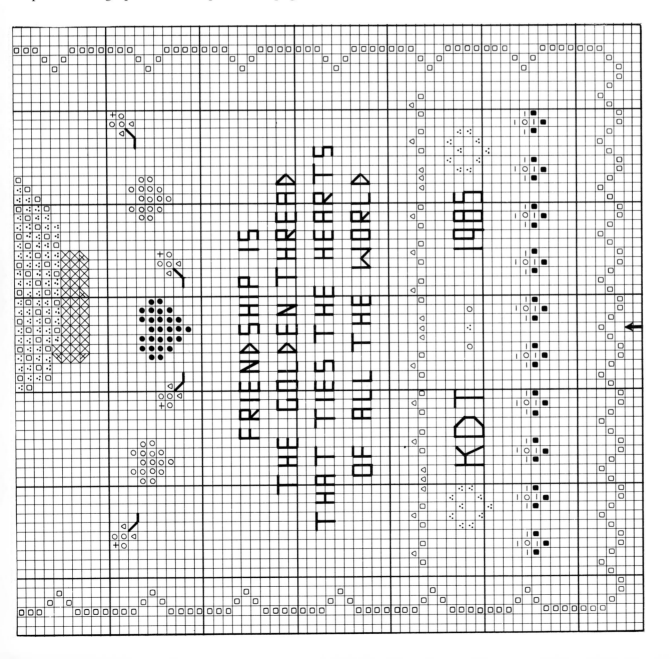

Thank you, God, for blessing us
with night and morning light—
dew and sun and friends to love.

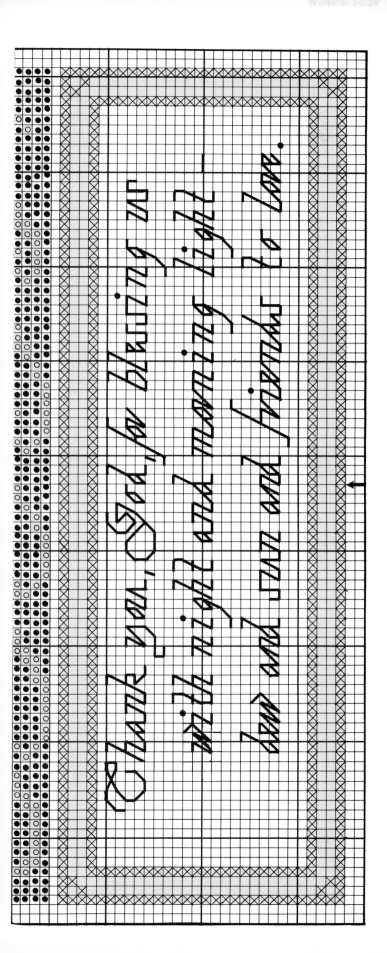

✓ A BIRD OF LOVE

Cover Sample: Stitched on White Hardanger 22 over two threads. Finished design size is 8″ × 10″. Cut fabric 14″ × 16″. Finished design sizes using other fabrics are: Aida 11 – 8″ × 10″; Aida 14 – 6¼″ × 7⅞″; Aida 18 – 4⅞″ × 6⅛″; Hardanger 22 – 4″ × 5″.

Bates		DMC	(used for cover sample)
			Step One: Cross-stitch (three strands)
1	·		White
886	▽	677	Old Gold - vy. lt.
921	●	931	Antique Blue - med.
875	✕	503	Blue Green - med.
878	▫	501	Blue Green - dk.
397	✕	453	Shell Gray - lt.
			Step Two: Filet Cross-stitch (one strand)
920	○	932	Antique Blue - lt.
875		503	Blue Green - med.
			Step Three: Back Stitch (one strand)
878		501	Blue Green - dk.
401		413	Pewter Gray - dk.
			Step Four: French Knots (one strand)
878	●	501	Blue Green - dk.

40

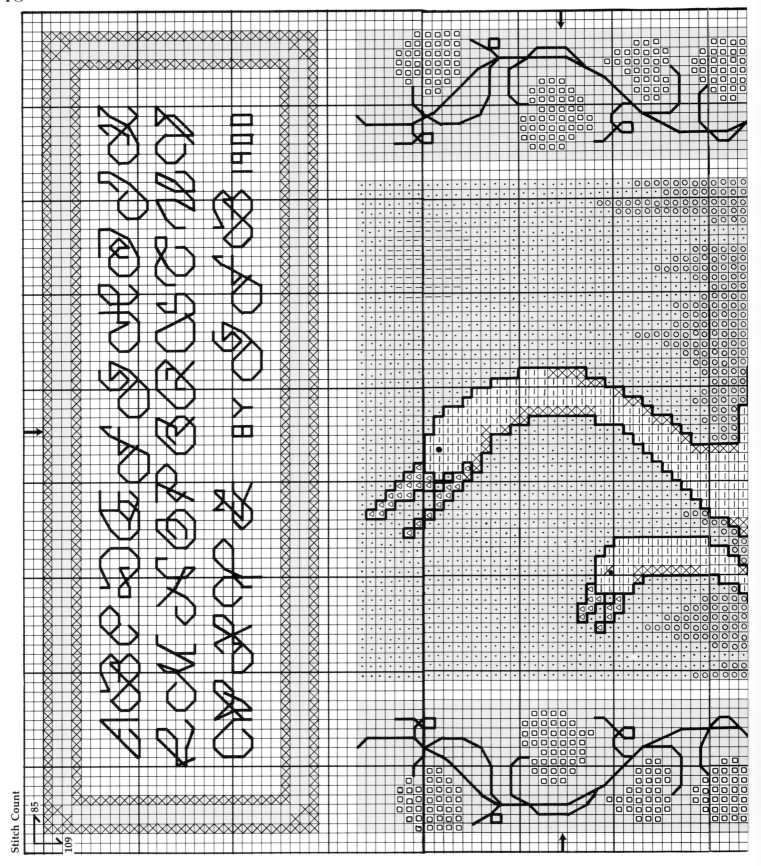

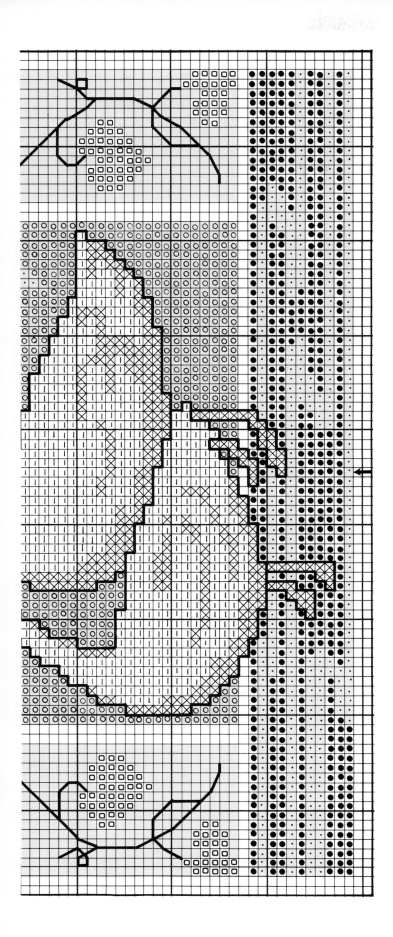

A LOVELY PAIR

Cover Sample: Stitched on White Hardanger 22 over two threads. Finished design size is 7¾" × 9⅞". Cut fabric 14" × 16". Finished design sizes using other fabrics are: Aida 11 – 7¾" × 9⅞"; Aida 14 – 6⅛" × 7¾"; Aida 18 – 4¾" × 6"; Hardanger 22 – 3⅞" × 5".

Bates		DMC (used for cover sample)	
		Step One: Cross-stitch (three strands)	
1	− ⁄		White
886	△	677	Old Gold - vy. lt.
921	● ⁄	931	Antique Blue - med.
213	✕	504	Blue Green - lt.
876	▢	502	Blue Green
397	✕	453	Shell Gray - lt.
		Step Two: Filet Cross-stitch (one strand)	
886	ı	677	Old Gold - vy. lt.
920	·	932	Antique Blue - lt.
213		504	Blue Green - lt.
878	○	501	Blue Green - dk.
		Step Three: Back Stitch (one strand)	
920		932	Antique Blue - lt. (name, date)
876		502	Blue Green (vines)
878		501	Blue Green - dk. (alphabet)
401		413	Pewter Gray - dk. (all else)

*God made the country,
    and man made the town.*

—William Cowper———————

✕ THE COUNTRYSIDE

Cover Sample: Stitched on White Hardanger 22 over two threads. Finished design size is 6⅜" × 8⅜". Cut fabric 13" × 15". Finished design sizes using other fabrics are: Aida 11 – 6⅜" × 8⅜"; Aida 14 – 5" × 6⅝"; Aida 18 – 3⅞" × 5⅛"; Hardanger 22 – 3⅛" × 4⅛".

Bates		DMC (used for cover sample)
		Step One: Cross-stitch (three strands)
926		Ecru
295	726	Topaz - lt.
306	725	Topaz
307	783	Christmas Gold
308	782	Topaz - med.
76	603	Cranberry
11	350	Coral - med.
13	349	Coral - dk.
46	321	Christmas Red
20	498	Christmas Red - dk.
95	554	Violet - lt.
101	550	Violet - vy. dk.
107	327	Antique Violet - dk.
128	800	Delft - pale
265	3348	Yellow Green - lt.
266	3347	Yellow Green - med.
215	368	Pistachio Green - lt.
206	955	Nile Green - lt.
203	954	Nile Green
210	562	Jade - med.
212	561	Jade - vy. dk.
879	890	Pistachio Green - ultra dk.
324	922	Copper - lt.
351	400	Mahogany - dk.
378	841	Beige Brown - lt.
357	801	Coffee Brown - dk.
380	838	Beige Brown - vy. dk.
398	415	Pearl Gray
		Step Two: Back Stitch (one strand)
307	783	Christmas Gold (two strands, grass)
382	3371	Black Brown (all else)

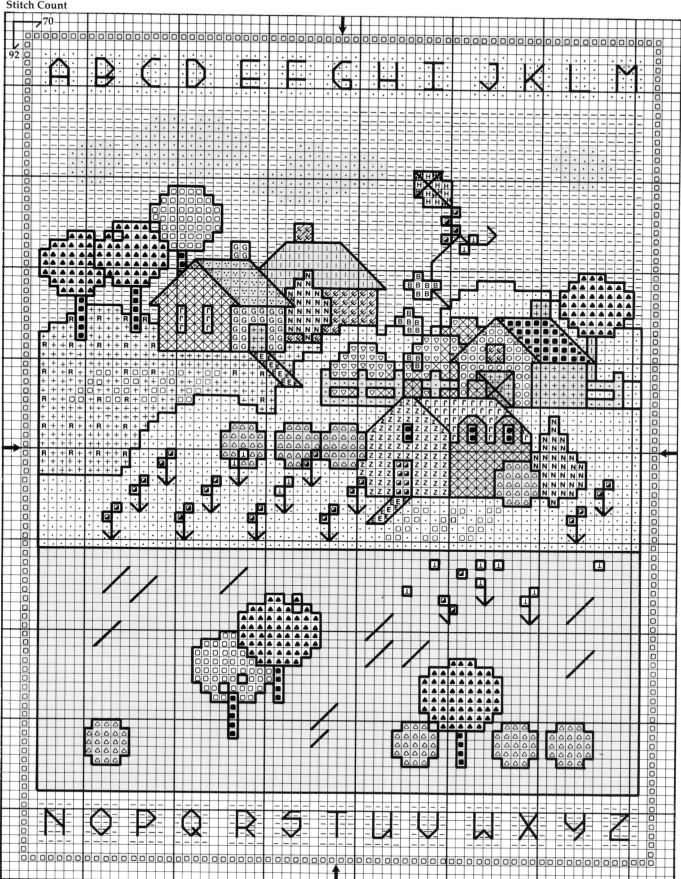

Stitch Count

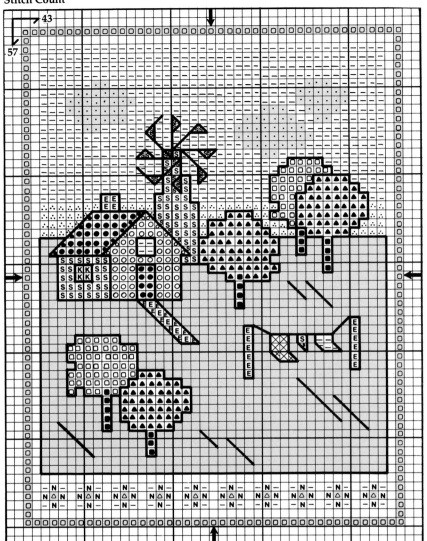

THE WINDMILL

Cover Sample: Stitched on White Hardanger 22 over two threads. Finished design size is 3⅞″ × 5⅛″. Cut fabric 10″ × 11″. Finished design sizes using other fabrics are: Aida 11 – 3⅞″ × 5⅛″; Aida 14 – 3⅛″ × 4⅛″; Aida 18 – 2″ × 3⅛″; Hardanger 22 – 2″ × 2⅝″.

Bates			DMC (used for cover sample)
			Step One: Cross-stitch (three strands)
926	·		Ecru
301	∴	⁄	744 Yellow - pale
306	▣		725 Topaz
307	✕	⁄	783 Christmas Gold
11	○	⁄	350 Coral - med.
47	s	⁄	304 Christmas Red - med.
128	–	⁄	800 Delft - pale
206	N		955 Nile Green - lt.
203	△		954 Nile Green
210	⁄		562 Jade - med.
212	▢		561 Jade - vy. dk.
879	▲		890 Pistachio Green - ultra dk.
324	E	⁄	922 Copper - lt.
5968	●	⁄	355 Terra Cotta - dk.
380	■		838 Beige Brown - vy. dk.
382	K		3371 Black Brown
			Step Two: Back Stitch (one strand)
307			783 Christmas Gold (two strands, grass)
382			3371 Black Brown (all else)

Stitch Count

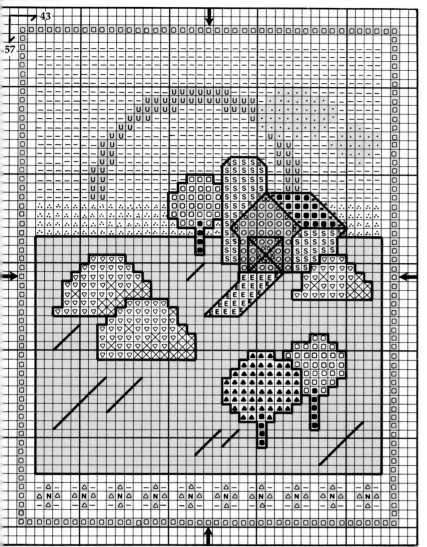

THE BARN

Cover Sample: Stitched on White Hardanger 22 over two threads. Finished design size is 3⅞″ × 5⅛″. Cut fabric 10″ × 11″. Finished design sizes using other fabrics are: Aida 11 – 3⅞″ × 5⅛″; Aida 14 – 3⅛″ × 4⅛″; Aida 18 – 2⅜″ × 3⅛″; Hardanger 22 – 2″ × 2⅝″.

Bates			DMC	(used for cover sample)
			Step One: Cross-stitch (three strands)	
926	·			Ecru
301	∴	◹	744	Yellow - pale
295	▽		726	Topaz - lt.
306	⊡		725	Topaz
307	✕		783	Christmas Gold
10	u		352	Coral - lt.
47	s	◸	304	Christmas Red - med.
43	⊙	◿	815	Garnet - med.
128	–		800	Delft - pale
206	N		955	Nile Green - lt.
203	△		954	Nile Green
210		◹	562	Jade - med.
212	☐		561	Jade - vy. dk.
879	▲		890	Pistachio Green - ultra dk.
324	E	◿	922	Copper - lt.
380	■	◿	838	Beige Brown - vy. dk.
			Step Two: Back Stitch (one strand)	
307			783	Christmas Gold (two strands, grass)
382			3371	Black Brown (all else)

Whole Wheat

FLOUR

All
Natural

THE JORGENSONS 1900

Dark brown is The river,
Golden is The sand
It flows along forever,
With trees on either hand.

—Robert Louis Stevenson

THE FLOUR SACK

Cover Sample: Stitched on Fiddler's Cloth 14. Finished design size is 10⅛" × 14⅞". Cut fabric 16" × 21". Finished design sizes using other fabrics are: Aida 11 – 12⅞" × 19"; Aida 14 – 10⅛" × 14⅞"; Aida 18 – 7⅛" × 11⅝"; Hardanger 22 – 6½" × 9½".

To personalize graph, refer to alphabet on page 161.

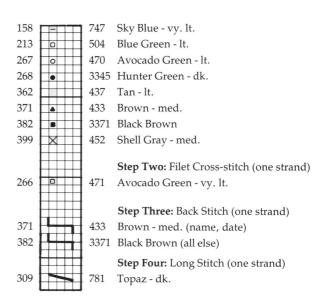

Bates		DMC (used for cover sample)	
		Step One: Cross-stitch (two strands)	
386		746	Off White
295		726	Topaz - lt.
305		725	Topaz
307		783	Christmas Gold
309		781	Topaz - dk.
347		977	Golden Brown - lt.
349		976	Golden Brown - med.
332		946	Burnt Orange - med.
19		817	Coral Red - vy. dk.

158		747	Sky Blue - vy. lt.
213		504	Blue Green - lt.
267		470	Avocado Green - lt.
268		3345	Hunter Green - dk.
362		437	Tan - lt.
371		433	Brown - med.
382		3371	Black Brown
399		452	Shell Gray - med.
		Step Two: Filet Cross-stitch (one strand)	
266		471	Avocado Green - vy. lt.
		Step Three: Back Stitch (one strand)	
371		433	Brown - med. (name, date)
382		3371	Black Brown (all else)
		Step Four: Long Stitch (one strand)	
309		781	Topaz - dk.

Stitch Count

142

209

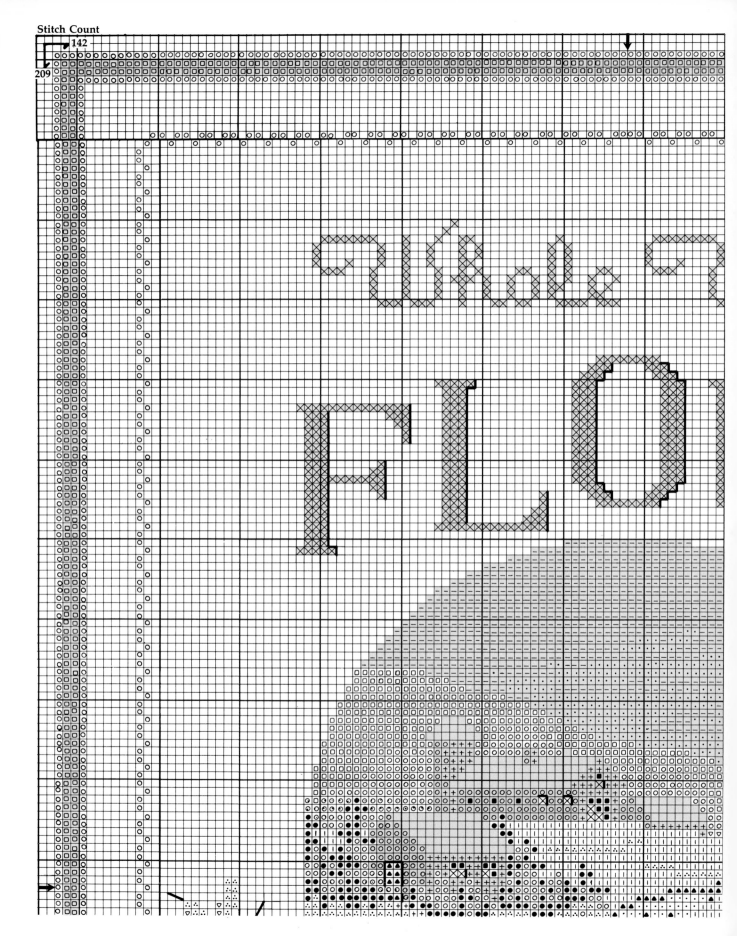

52

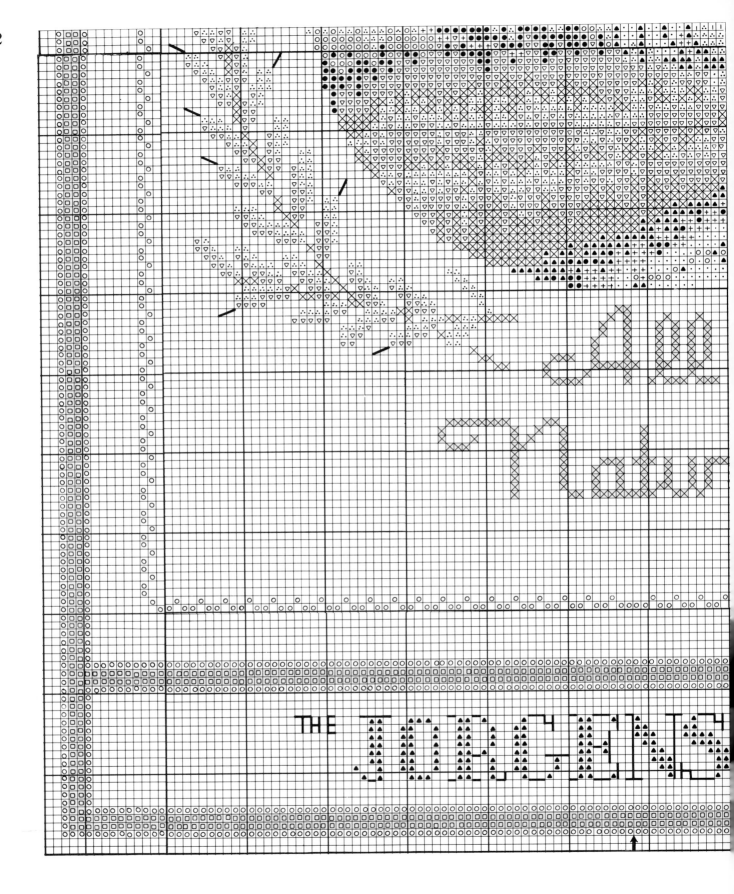

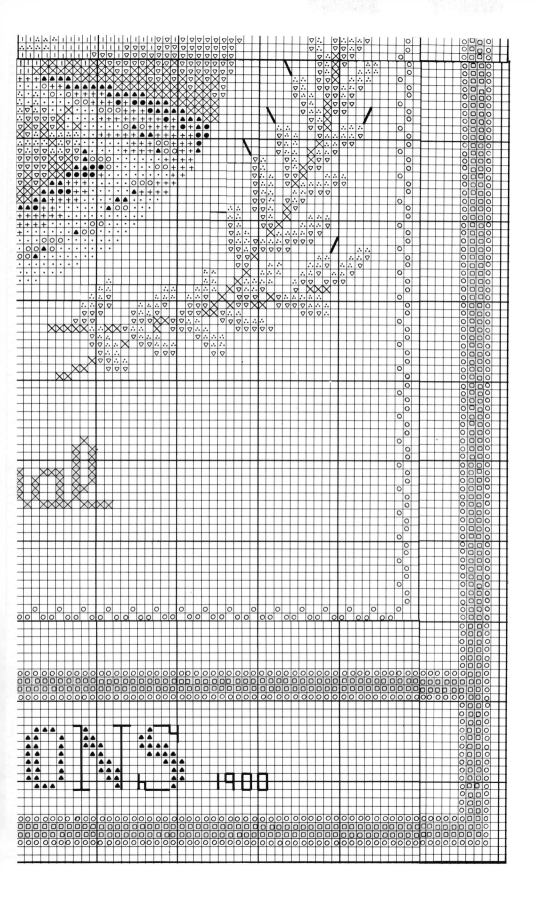

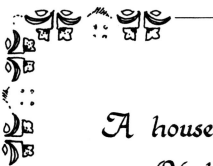

54

A house is built of logs and stone,
Of tiles and posts and piers;
A home is built of loving deeds
That stand a thousand years.

—Victor Hugo—

Satin Stitch

Satin Stitch

Outline Stitch

French Knots: one wrap with two strands

Lazy Daisy Stitch

Lazy Daisy Stitch

Satin Stitch

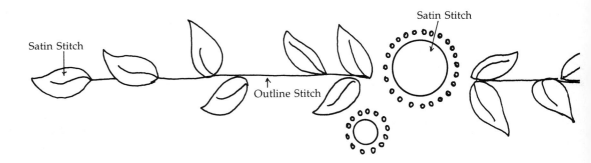

● Match to dot on page 58.

WELCOME

Cover Sample: Stitched on unbleached muslin. Finished design size is 18½″ × 15¾″. Cut fabric 26″ × 24″. Two strands of cream candlewicking thread are used throughout, except as indicated for some French knots. See General Instructions for Candlewicking on page 166.

Ribbon work: 3 yards of ¼″ wide cream satin ribbon. Cut one 13″ length to be couched with blanket stitch below "Welcome." Cut remaining ribbon into four equal lengths. For ribbon border, draw line with dressmaker's pen 1¼″ outside widest points of design. Pin ribbon outside lines, overlapping ribbon at each corner. Couch with straight stitch and French knots at ¾″ intervals; see Diagram 1.

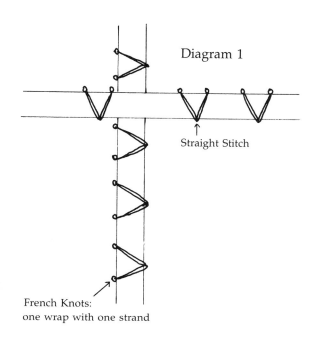

Diagram 1

Straight Stitch

French Knots:
one wrap with one strand

French Knots: one wrap with one strand

Satin Stitch

Outline Stitch

Match to dot on page 59. ●

58

●Match to dot on page 56.

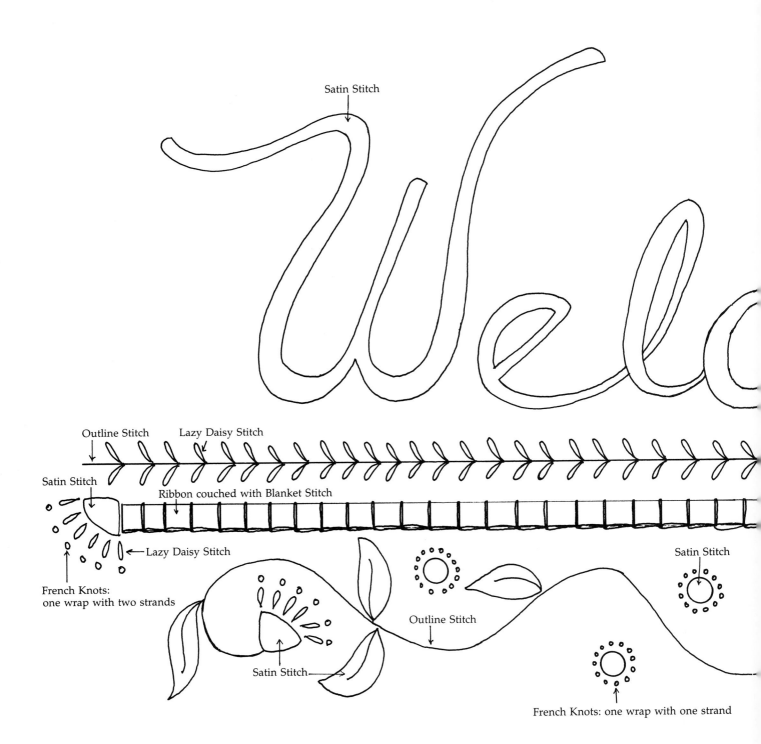

Satin Stitch

Outline Stitch

Lazy Daisy Stitch

Satin Stitch

Ribbon couched with Blanket Stitch

Lazy Daisy Stitch

French Knots:
one wrap with two strands

Satin Stitch

Outline Stitch

Satin Stitch

French Knots: one wrap with one strand

Match to dot on page 57.●

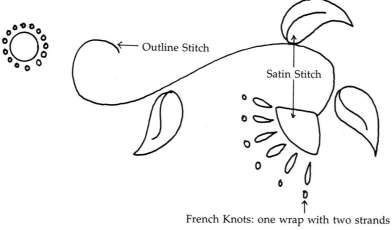

Outline Stitch

Satin Stitch

French Knots: one wrap with two strands

He who loves an old house
never loves in vain.

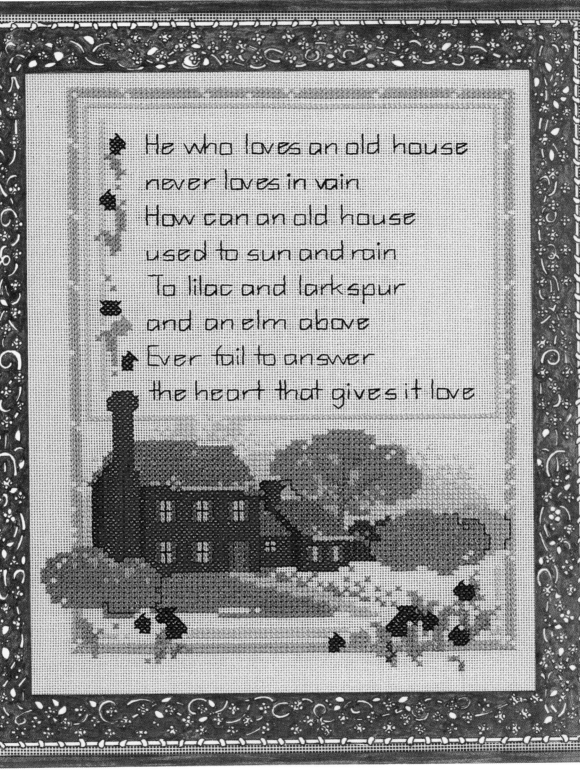

62

116

91

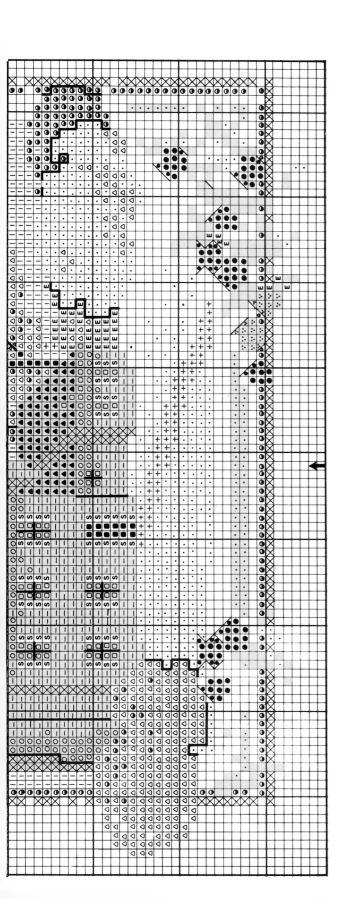

AN OLD HOUSE

Cover Sample: Stitched on White Linda 27 over two threads. Finished design size is 6¼″ × 8⅝″. Cut fabric 13″ × 15″. Finished design sizes using other fabrics are: Aida 11 – 8¼″ × 10½″; Aida 14 – 6½″ × 8¼″; Aida 18 – 5″ × 6½″; Hardanger 22 – 4⅛″ × 5¼″.

Bates		DMC	(used for cover sample)
			Step One: Cross-stitch (two strands)
20		498	Christmas Red - dk.
43		815	Garnet - med.
44		814	Garnet - dk.
108		211	Lavender - lt.
95		554	Violet - lt.
101		550	Violet - vy. dk.
158		828	Blue Ultra - vy. lt.
131		798	Delft - dk.
167		598	Turquoise - lt.
168		597	Turquoise
186		959	Seagreen - med.
187		958	Seagreen - dk.
187		992	Aquamarine
189		991	Aquamarine - dk.
376		842	Beige Brown - vy. lt.
379		840	Beige Brown - med.
397		453	Shell Gray - lt.
399		451	Shell Gray - dk.
			Step Two: Back Stitch (one strand)
44		814	Garnet - dk. (house)
189		991	Aquamarine - dk. (grass)
379		840	Beige Brown - med. (trees)
381		938	Coffee Brown - ultra dk. (all else)
			Step Three: French Knots (one strand)
381		938	Coffee Brown - ultra dk. (poem)

A little garden in which to walk
and immensity in which to dream.

A little garden in which to walk and immensity in which to dream.

Stitch Count

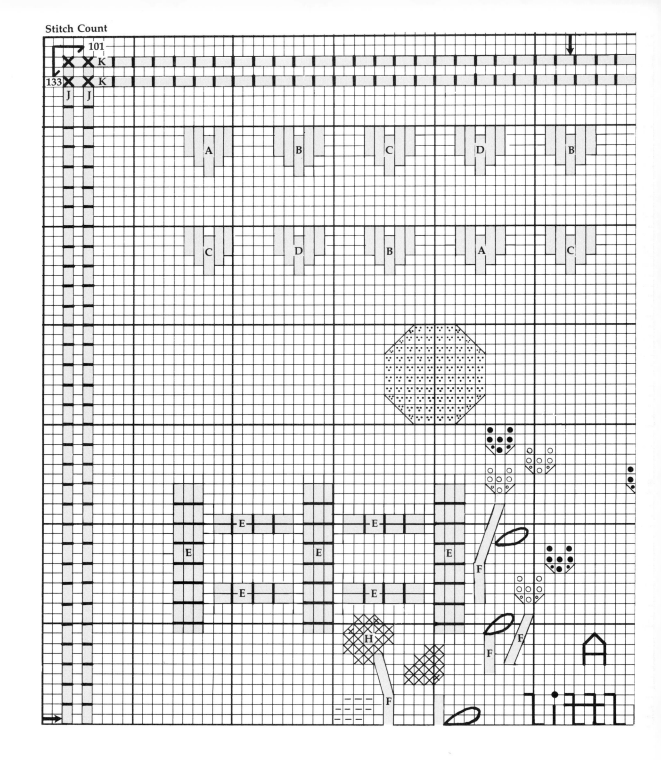

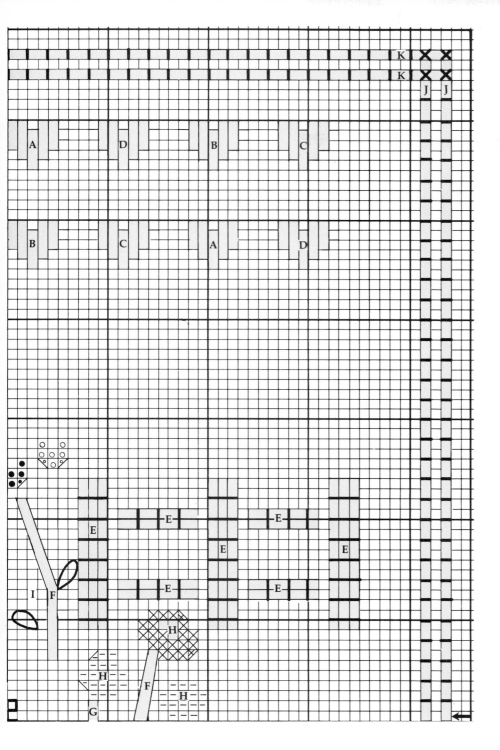

A LITTLE GARDEN

Cover Sample: Stitched on White Hardanger 22 over two threads. Finished design size is 9⅛″ × 12⅛″. Cut fabric 15″ × 18″.

Also needed:
  ¾ yd. ¹⁄₁₆″ wide light pink satin ribbon
  ¾ yd. ¹⁄₁₆″ wide pink satin ribbon
  1 ⅞ yds. ¹⁄₁₆″ wide lavender satin ribbon
  ¾ yd. ¹⁄₁₆″ wide peach satin ribbon
  2 ¾ yds. ¹⁄₁₆″ wide rose satin ribbon; matching thread
  2 ½ yds. ¹⁄₁₆″ wide light green satin ribbon; matching thread
  ¾ yd. ¹⁄₁₆″ wide dark green satin ribbon; matching thread
  1 yd. ¹⁄₁₆″ wide yellow satin ribbon
  3 yds. ¹⁄₁₆″ wide blue satin ribbon; matching thread
Large-eyed needle

Bates			DMC	(used for cover sample)
			Step One:	Cross-stitch (two strands)
292	∴	◢	3078	Golden Yellow - vy. lt.
8	✕	◢	353	Peach Flesh
10		◢	352	Coral - lt.
24	○	◢	776	Pink - med.
27	●	◢	899	Rose - med.
108	+	◢	211	Lavender - lt.
			Step Two:	Back Stitch (one strand)
210	⌐		562	Jade - med.
			Step Three:	French Knots
210	●		562	Jade - med. (one strand)

Step Four: Ribbon Work
Using ribbons A – D, satin stitch hearts

A. light pink
B. pink
C. lavender
D. peach
E. Using rose ribbon, satin stitch fence; couch with matching thread.
F. Using light green ribbon, sew straight stitches for stems, making loops for leaves; couch stems with matching thread and tack loops.

For ribbon work, individual couching lines are indicated on graph.

(Continued on page 69)

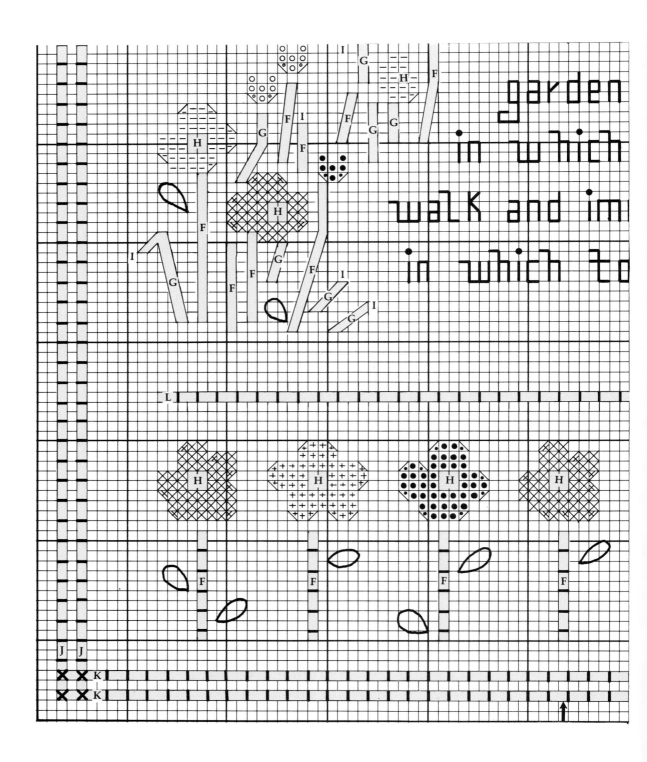

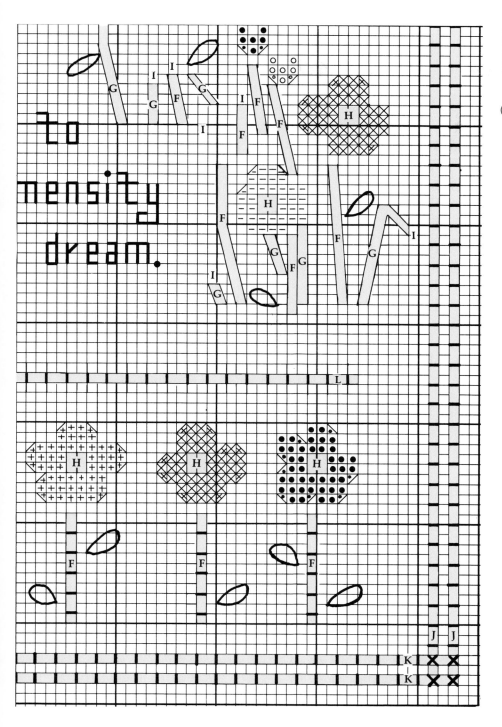

to
mensity
dream.

A LITTLE GARDEN

(Continued from page 67)

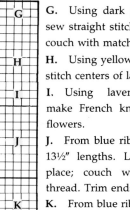

G. Using dark green ribbon, sew straight stitches for stems; couch with matching thread.

H. Using yellow ribbon, satin stitch centers of large flowers.

I. Using lavender ribbon, make French knots for small flowers.

J. From blue ribbon, cut four 13½" lengths. Lay ribbon in place; couch with matching thread. Trim ends.

K. From blue ribbon, cut four 10½" lengths. Lay ribbons in place; couch with matching thread. Trim ends. Sew cross-stitches over ribbons.

L. Lay remaining blue ribbon in place. Thread ribbon ends to WRONG side and tack; couch with matching thread.

For ribbon work, individual couching lines are indicated on graph.

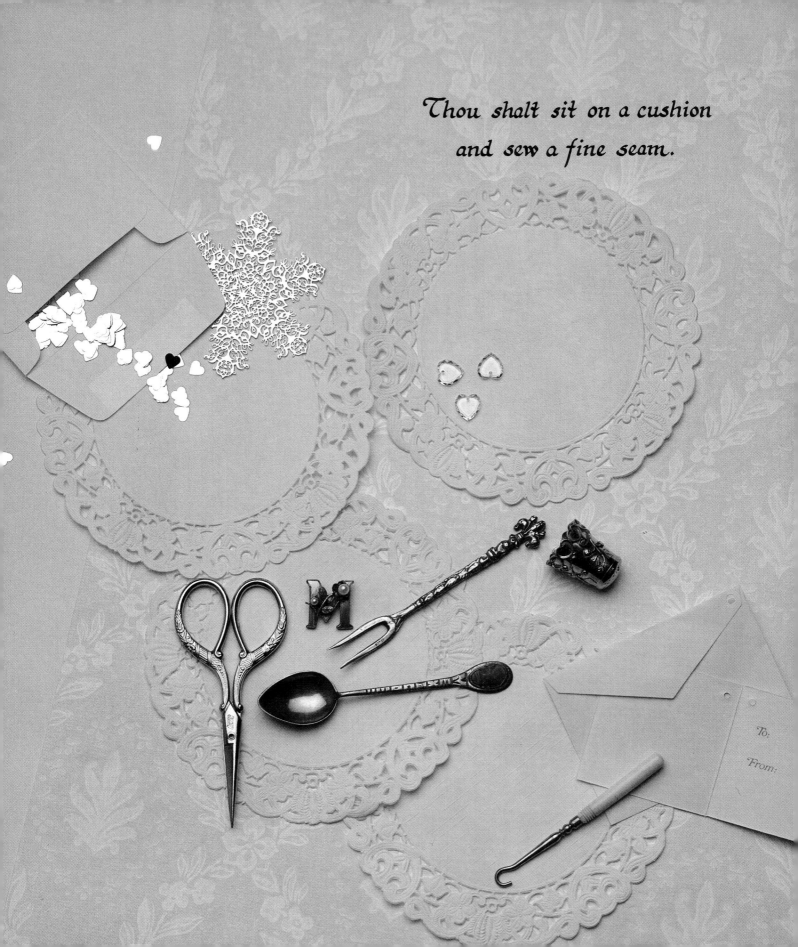

Thou shalt sit on a cushion
and sew a fine seam.

Thou shalt sit on a cushion
and sew a fine seam,

And feed upon strawberries,
sugar and cream.

Stitch Count

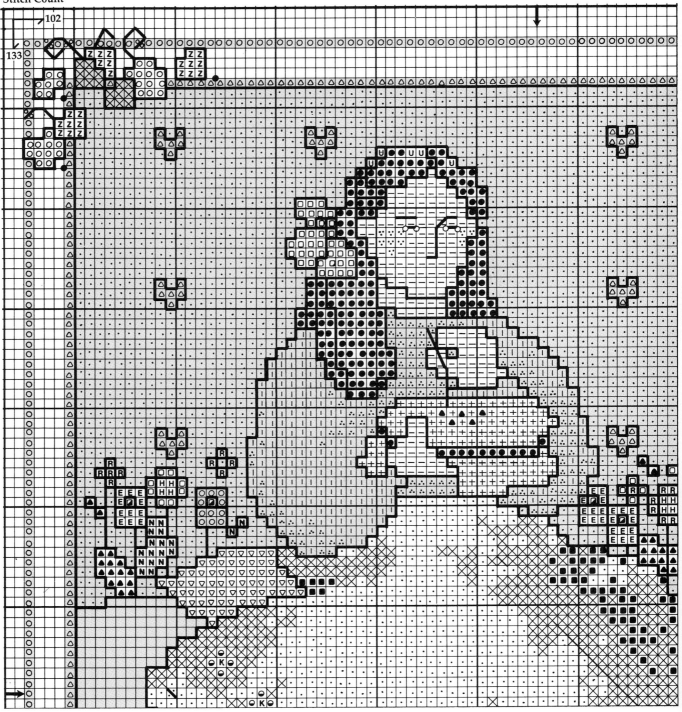

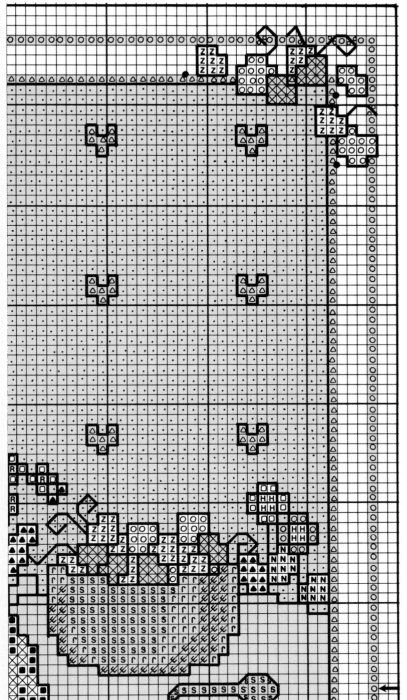

SEW A FINE SEAM

Cover Sample: Stitched on White Belfast Linen 32 over two threads. Finished design size is 6⅜″ × 8¼″. Cut fabric 13″ × 14″. Finished design sizes using other fabrics are: Aida 11 – 9¼″ × 12⅛″; Aida 14 – 7 ¼″ × 9½″; Aida 18 – 5⅝″ × 7⅜″; Hardanger 22 – 4⅝″ × 6″.

Bates		DMC (used for cover sample)	
		Step One: Cross-stitch (two strands)	
1	+		White
886	R	677	Old Gold - vy. lt.
301	H	744	Yellow - pale
301	K	744	Yellow - pale (bead over cross-stitch)
778	·	754	Peach Flesh - lt.
868	X	758	Terra Cotta - lt.
5975	■	356	Terra Cotta - med.
49	o	3689	Mauve - lt.
76	△	962	Dusty Rose - med.
893	∵	224	Shell Pink - lt.
9	□	760	Salmon
42	z	309	Rose - deep
59	X	326	Rose - vy. deep
59	⊘	326	Rose - vy. deep (bead over cross-stitch)
108	E	211	Lavender - lt.
95	▣	554	Violet - lt.
118	i	340	Blue Violet - med.
119	∴	333	Blue Violet - dk.
158	+	775	Baby Blue - lt.
159	□	3325	Baby Blue
875	N	503	Blue Green - med.
876	/	502	Blue Green
208	o	563	Jade - lt.
212	▲	561	Jade - vy. dk.
933	−	543	Beige Brown - ultra vy. lt.
942	▽	738	Tan - vy. lt.
882	U	407	Sportsman Flesh - dk.
936	●	632	Negro Flesh
397	S	762	Pearl Gray - vy. lt.
398	ſ	415	Pearl Gray
399	≪	318	Steel Gray - lt.

(Continued on page 75)

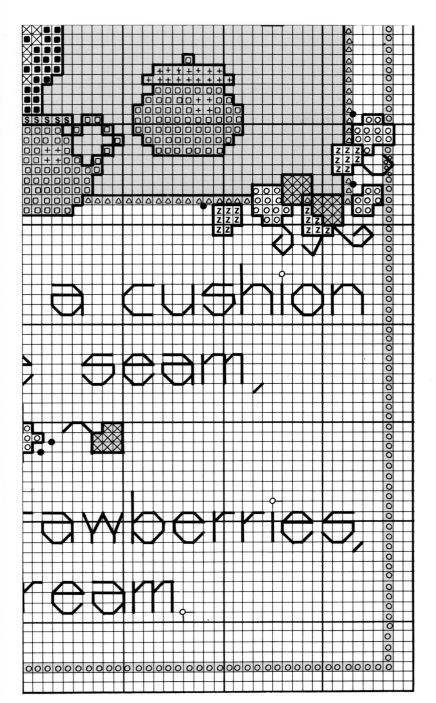

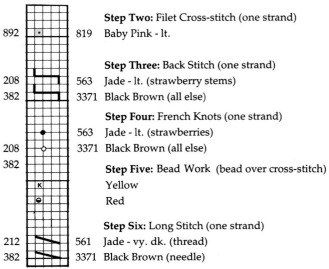

SEW A FINE SEAM

(Continued from page 73)

892		819	**Step Two:** Filet Cross-stitch (one strand) Baby Pink - lt.
			Step Three: Back Stitch (one strand)
208		563	Jade - lt. (strawberry stems)
382		3371	Black Brown (all else)
			Step Four: French Knots (one strand)
		563	Jade - lt. (strawberries)
208		3371	Black Brown (all else)
382			
			Step Five: Bead Work (bead over cross-stitch)
	K		Yellow
			Red
			Step Six: Long Stitch (one strand)
212		561	Jade - vy. dk. (thread)
382		3371	Black Brown (needle)

I was raised on the farm. My mother said that milking cows would make my fingers strong for playing the piano.

—Marla Stutz———

MILK AND HONEY

WINE AND CHEESE

MILK AND HONEY

Cover Sample: Stitched on White Hardanger 22 over two threads. Finished design size is 5⅝″ × 6″. Cut fabric 11½″ × 12″. Finished design sizes using other fabrics are: Aida 11 – 5⅝″ × 6″; Aida 14 – 4½″ × 4¾″; Aida 18 – 3½″ × 3⅝″; Hardanger 22 – 2⅞″ × 3″.

Cover Sample: Stitched on White Hardanger 22 over two threads. Finished design size is 5⅝″ × 6″. Cut fabric 11½″ × 12″. Finished design sizes using other fabrics are: Aida 11 – 5⅝″ × 6″; Aida 14 – 4½″ × 4¾″; Aida 18 – 3½″ × 3⅝″; Hardanger 22 – 2⅞″ × 3″.

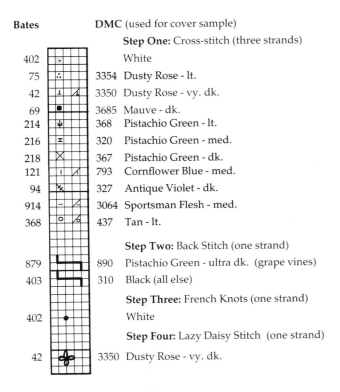

WINE AND CHEESE

Bates	DMC (used for cover sample)	
		Step One: Cross-stitch (three strands)
402		White
75	3354	Dusty Rose - lt.
42	3350	Dusty Rose - vy. dk.
69	3685	Mauve - dk.
214	368	Pistachio Green - lt.
216	320	Pistachio Green - med.
218	367	Pistachio Green - dk.
121	793	Cornflower Blue - med.
94	327	Antique Violet - dk.
914	3064	Sportsman Flesh - med.
368	437	Tan - lt.
		Step Two: Back Stitch (one strand)
879	890	Pistachio Green - ultra dk. (grape vines)
403	310	Black (all else)
		Step Three: French Knots (one strand)
402		White
		Step Four: Lazy Daisy Stitch (one strand)
42	3350	Dusty Rose - vy. dk.

MILK AND HONEY

Bates	DMC (used for cover sample)	
		Step One: Cross-stitch (three strands)
402		White
75	3354	Dusty Rose - lt.
44	816	Garnet
214	368	Pistachio Green - lt.
216	320	Pistachio Green - med.
218	367	Pistachio Green - dk.
121	793	Cornflower Blue - med.
914	3064	Sportsman Flesh - med.
368	437	Tan - lt.
369	435	Brown - vy. lt.
		Step Two: Back Stitch (one strand)
403	310	Black
		Step Three: French Knots (one strand)
402		White
		Step Four: Lazy Daisy Stitch (one strand)
44	816	Garnet (flowers on cow)
403	310	Black (bees)

WINE AND CHEESE

Stitch Count

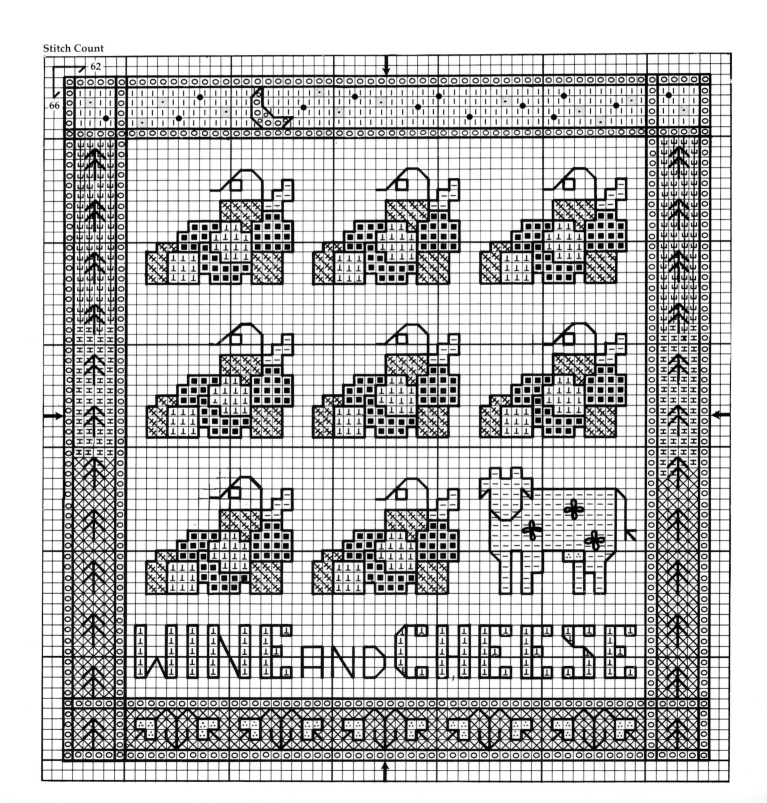

MILK AND HONEY

Stitch Count

Nature itself
tells us what to eat.

—A Creole Saying—

84

Stitch Count

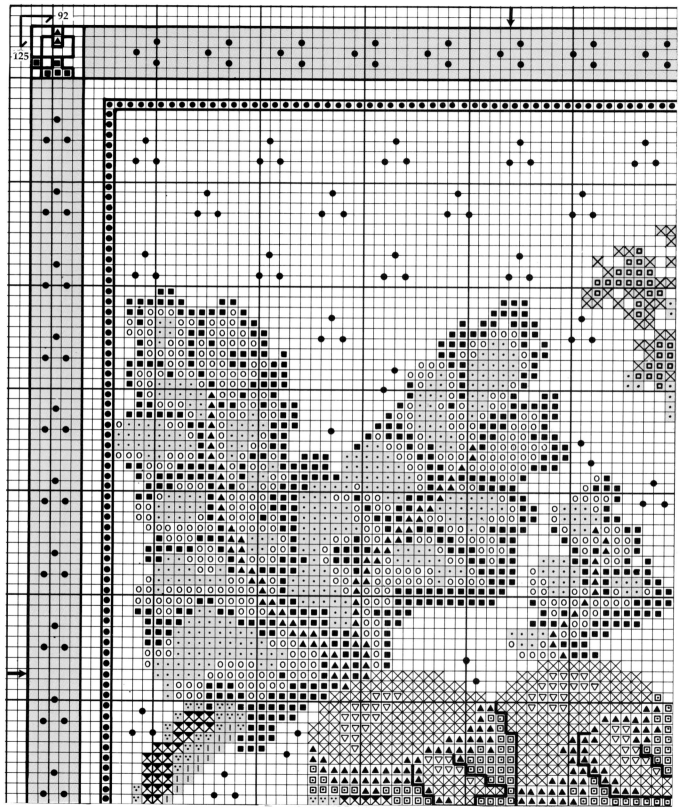

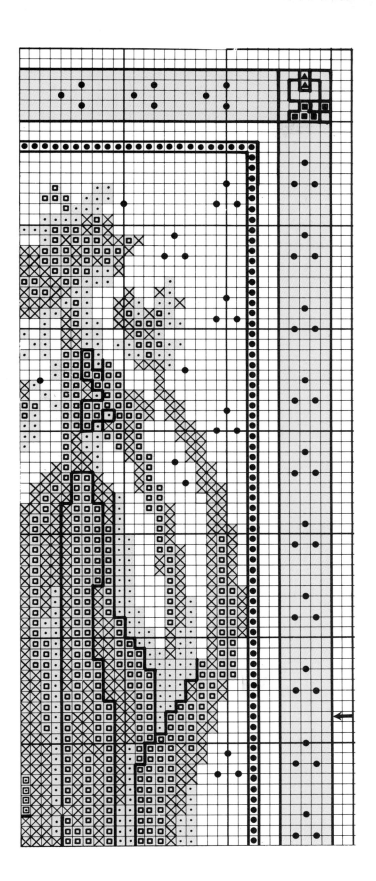

✓ AUTUMN HARVEST

Cover Sample: Stitched on Cream Linda 27. Finished design size is 6¾" × 9¼". Cut fabric 13" × 15". Finished design sizes using other fabrics are: Aida 11 – 8⅜" × 11⅜"; Aida 14 – 6⅝" × 8⅞"; Aida 18 – 5⅛" × 7"; Hardanger 22 – 4⅛" × 5⅝".

Bates		DMC	(used for cover sample)
			Step One: Cross-stitch (two strands)
386	−	746	Off White
292	·	3078	Golden Yellow - vy. lt.
306	✕	725	Topaz
893	⦂	224	Shell Pink - lt.
46	✔	666	Christmas Red - bright
47	▽	321	Christmas Red
47	✕	304	Christmas Red - med.
43	▲	815	Garnet - med.
72	⊡	902	Garnet - vy. lt.
264	□	772	Pine Green - lt.
242	✕	989	Forest Green
243	·	988	Forest Green - med.
246	○	986	Forest Green - vy. dk.
879	■	890	Pistachio Green - ultra dk.
307	⦂	977	Golden Brown - lt.
308	I	976	Golden Brown - med.
362		437	Tan - lt.
357	●	801	Coffee Brown - dk.
			Step Two: Back Stitch (one strand)
72		902	Garnet - vy. dk. (between beets and tomatoes)
246		986	Forest Green - vy. dk. (celery)
357		801	Coffee Brown - dk. (borders)
			Step Three: French Knots (one strand)
341	●	918	Red Copper - dk.

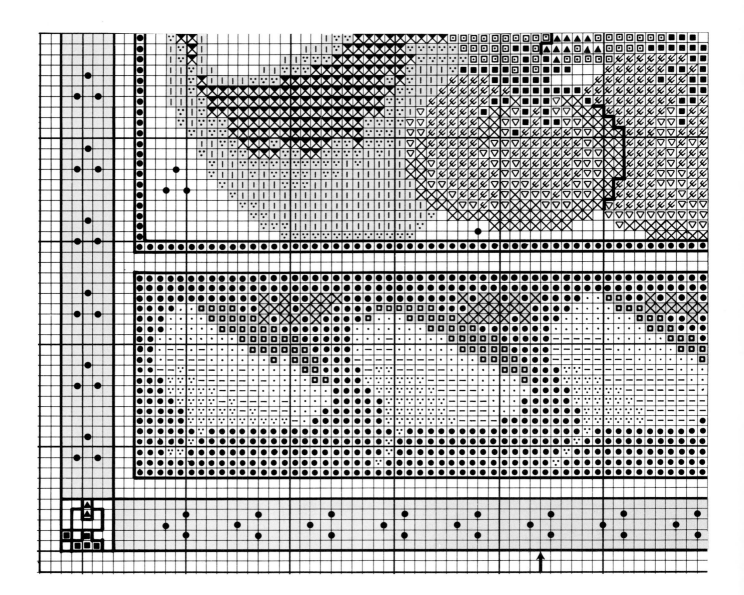

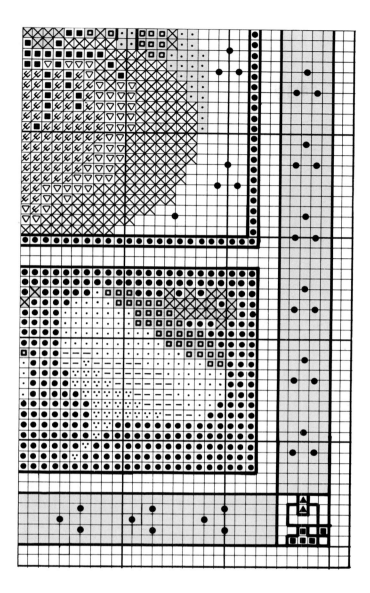

AUTUMN HARVEST

Cover Sample: Stitched on Cream Linda 27. Finished design size is 6¾″ × 9¼″. Cut fabric 13″ × 15″. Finished design sizes using other fabrics are: Aida 11 – 8⅜″ × 11⅜″; Aida 14 – 6⅝″ × 8⅞″; Aida 18 – 5⅛″ × 7″; Hardanger 22 – 4⅛″ × 5⅝″.

Bates		DMC (used for cover sample)	
		Step One: Cross-stitch (two strands)	
386	–	746	Off White
292	·	3078	Golden Yellow - vy. lt.
306	⊠	725	Topaz
893	⋰	224	Shell Pink - lt.
46	⚡	666	Christmas Red - bright
47	▽	321	Christmas Red
47	✕	304	Christmas Red - med.
43	▲	815	Garnet - med.
72	◙	902	Garnet - vy. lt.
264	□	772	Pine Green - lt.
242	✕	989	Forest Green
243	⋮	988	Forest Green - med.
246	○	986	Forest Green - vy. dk.
879	■	890	Pistachio Green - ultra dk.
307	⋰	977	Golden Brown - lt.
308	I	976	Golden Brown - med.
362		437	Tan - lt.
357	●	801	Coffee Brown - dk.
		Step Two: Back Stitch (one strand)	
72		902	Garnet - vy. dk. (between beets and tomatoes)
246		986	Forest Green - vy. dk. (celery)
357		801	Coffee Brown - dk. (borders)
		Step Three: French Knots (one strand)	
341	●	918	Red Copper - dk.

God's gifts

put man's best dreams

to shame.

—Elizabeth Barrett Browning—

Stitch Count

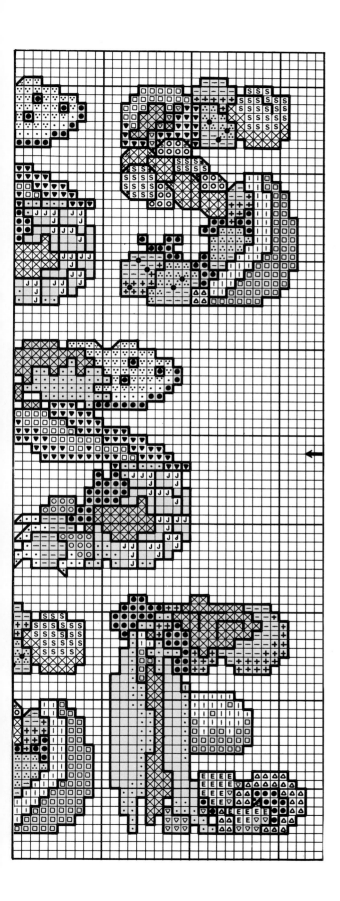

BLESS THIS HOUSE

Cover Sample: Stitched on White Hardanger 22 over two threads. Finished design size is 10⅜″ × 8″. Cut fabric 17″ × 14″. Finished design sizes using other fabrics are: Aida 11 – 10⅜″ × 8″; Aida 14 – 8⅛″ × 6¼″; Aida 18 – 6⅜″ × 4⅞″; Hardanger 22 – 5⅛″ × 4″.

Bates			DMC	(used for cover sample)
			Step One: Cross-stitch (three strands)	
1	·	◿		White
926	J			Ecru
300	I	◿	745	Yellow - lt. pale
323	□		722	Orange Spice - lt.
324	▼	◿	721	Orange Spice - med.
11	⋰		350	Coral - med.
19	−	◿	817	Coral Red - vy. dk.
43	o	◿	815	Garnet - med.
20	+	◿	498	Christmas Red - dk.
26	+		3708	Melon - lt.
28	⋰	◿	3706	Melon - med.
86	s	◿	3608	Plum - vy. lt.
98	✕		553	Violet - med.
101	o	◿	327	Antique Violet - dk.
206		◿	955	Nile Green - lt.
208	·	◿	563	Jade - lt.
210	✕	◿	562	Jade - med.
212	●	◿	561	Jade - vy. dk.
891	□		676	Old Gold - lt.
362	△	◿	437	Tan - lt.
914	E	◿	3064	Sportsman Flesh - med.
936	▽	◿	632	Negro Flesh
382	●	◿	3371	Black Brown
			Step Two: Back Stitch (one strand)	
403	⌐		310	Black
			Step Three: French Knots (one strand)	
382	◆		3371	Black Brown

The events of childhood do not pass,
but repeat Themselves like seasons of The year.

—Eleanor Farjeon——

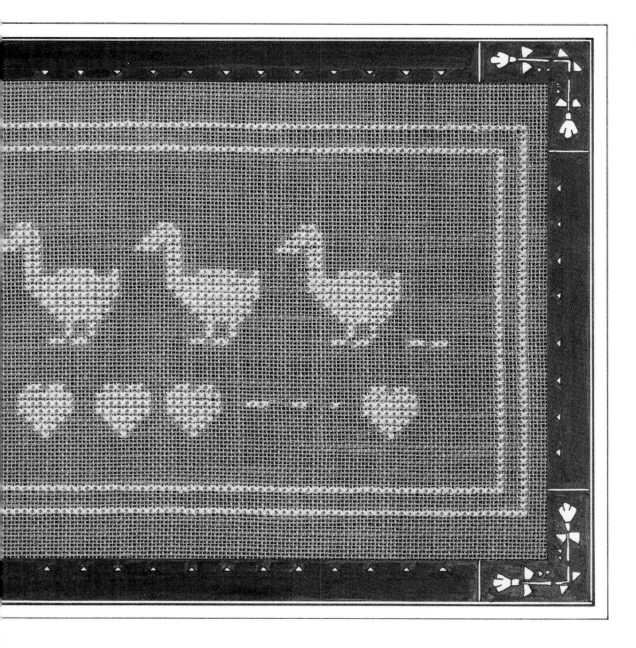

ALL IN A ROW

Cover Sample: Stitched on Brown Linen 25 over two threads. Finished design size is 9⅞" × 4⅛". For finished design sizes using other fabrics, divide stitch count of design by thread count of fabric.

Bates		DMC (used for cover sample)

Step One: Cross-stitch (two strands)

387 | 712 Cream

Stitch Count for Option

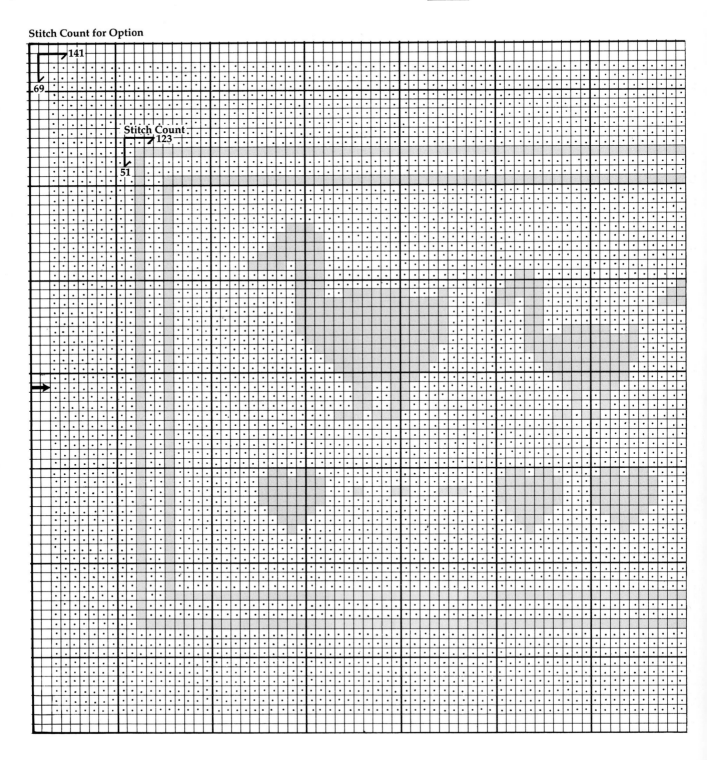

Filet Cross-stitch Option: Stitched on Brown Linen 25 over two threads. Finished design size is 11¼″ × 5⅛″. Cut fabric 18″ ×12″. For finished design sizes using other fabrics, divide stitch count of design by thread count of fabric.

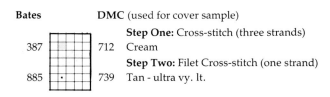

Bates		DMC (used for cover sample)
		Step One: Cross-stitch (three strands)
387		712 Cream
		Step Two: Filet Cross-stitch (one strand)
885		739 Tan - ultra vy. lt.

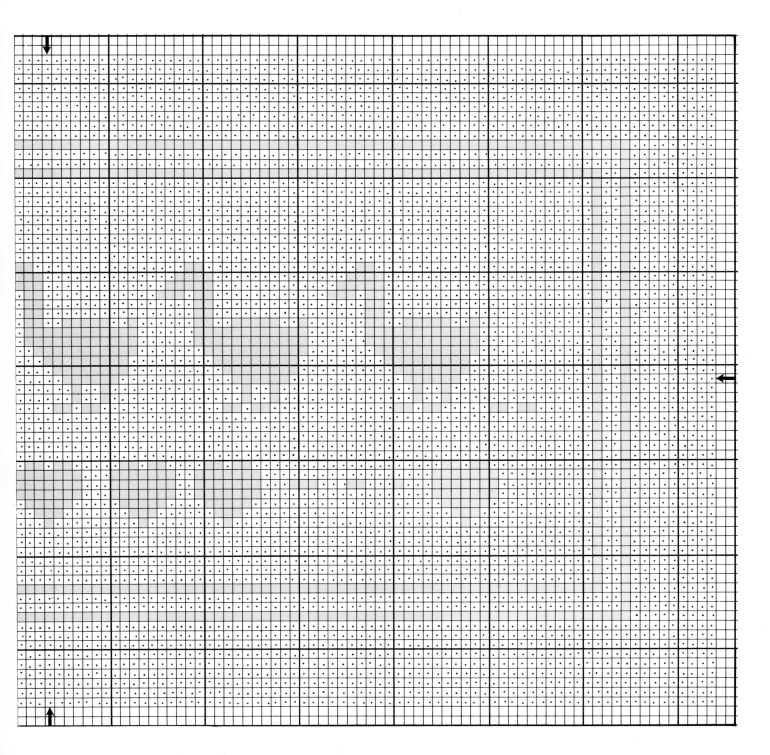

Son, Brother,
Husband, Father, Friend,
and Man.

I've six complete successes to become
Before the end of this, my mortal span.
God help me to excel in every one,
Son, Brother, Husband, Father, Friend
and Man.

FOR J.C.B. FROM J.K.T. 1984

Stitch Count

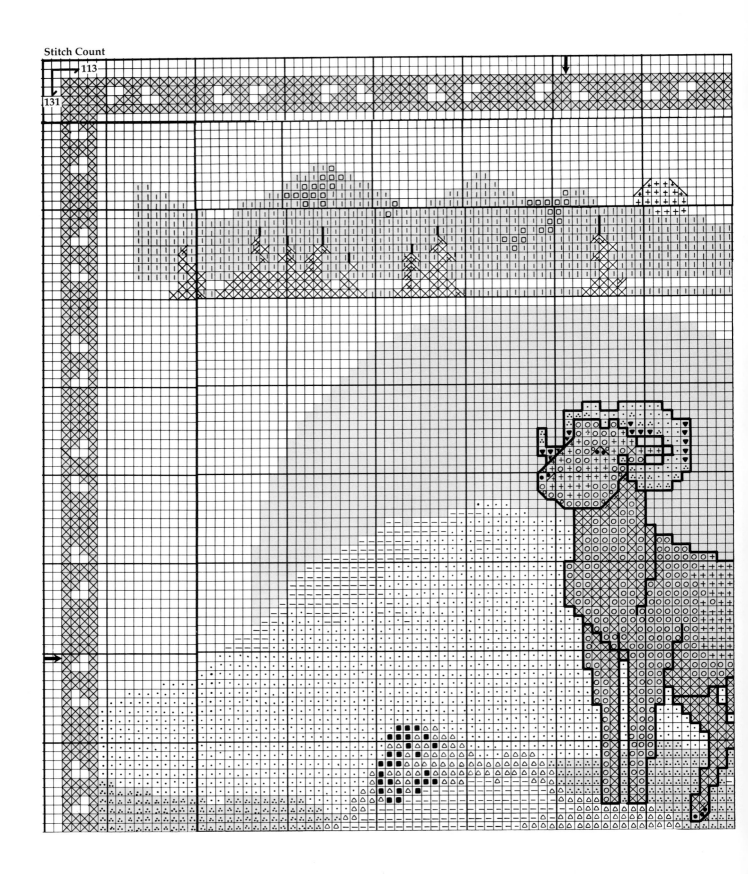

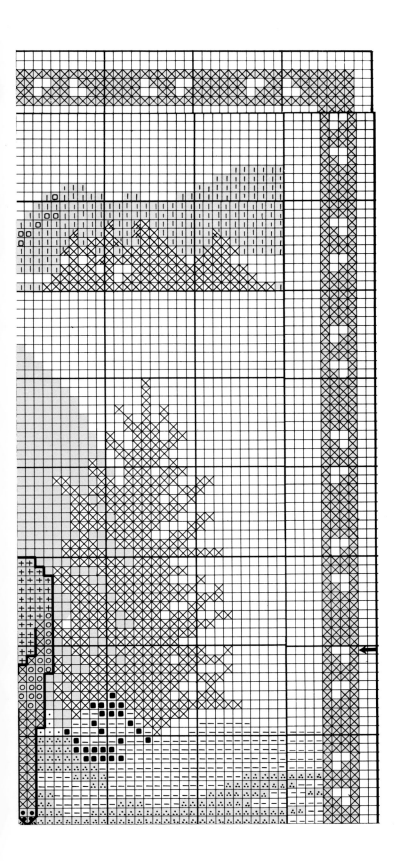

THE BIG HORN SHEEP

Cover Sample: Stitched on Cream Hardanger 22 over two threads. Finished design size is 10¼″ × 11⅞″. Cut fabric 17″ × 18″. Finished design sizes using other fabrics are: Aida 11 – 10¼″ × 11⅞″; Aida 14 – 8⅛″ × 9⅜″; Aida 18 – 6¼″ × 7¼″; Hardanger 22 – 5⅛″ × 6″.

Bates			DMC	(used for cover sample)
				Step One: Cross-stitch (three strands)
1	=			White
869	ı	⁄	3042	Antique Violet - lt.
871	□		3041	Antique Violet - med.
158		⁄	828	Blue Ultra - vy. lt.
876	·		502	Blue Green
246	✕	⁄	319	Pistachio Green - vy. dk.
886	·		3047	Yellow Beige - lt.
887	∴	⁄	3046	Yellow Beige - med.
373	▼	⁄	3045	Yellow Beige - dk.
387	+		822	Beige Gray - lt.
830	○	⁄	644	Beige Gray - med.
903	⊠	⁄	640	Beige Gray - vy. dk.
382	●		3371	Black Brown
398	△		415	Pearl Gray
400	■		414	Steel Gray - dk.
				Step Two: Filet Cross-stitch (one strand)
301	+	⁄	744	Yellow - pale
387	○	⁄	822	Beige Gray - lt.
				Step Three: Back Stitch (one strand)
246			319	Pistachio Green - vy. dk. (two strands)
				(trees)
246			319	Pistachio Green - vy. dk. (name, date)
382			3371	Black Brown (all else)
				Step Four: French Knots (one strand)
246	●		319	Pistachio Green - vy. dk. (initials)
382	○		3371	Black Brown (all else)

To personalize graph, refer to alphabet on page 162.

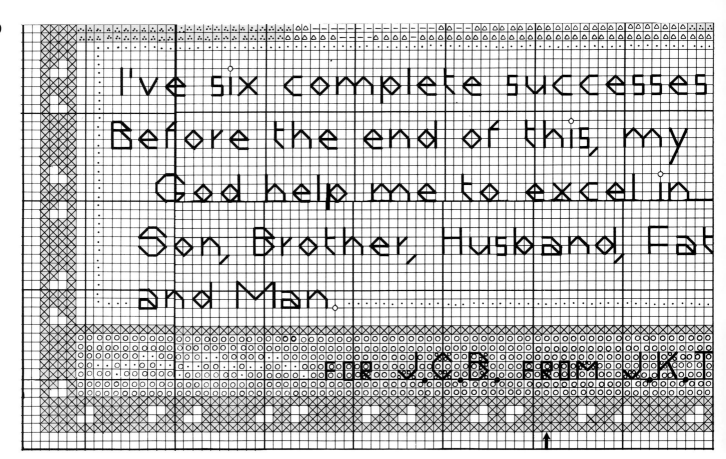

to become
mortal span,
every one,
her, Friend

THE BIG HORN SHEEP

Cover Sample: Stitched on Cream Hardanger 22 over two threads. Finished design size is 10¼″ × 11⅞″. Cut fabric 17″ × 18″. Finished design sizes using other fabrics are: Aida 11 – 10¼″ × 11⅞″; Aida 14 – 8⅛″ × 9⅜″; Aida 18 – 6¼″ × 7¼″; Hardanger 22 – 5⅛″ × 6″.

Bates		DMC (used for cover sample)
		Step One: Cross-stitch (three strands)
1	–	White
869	∣ ╱	3042 Antique Violet - lt.
871	□	3041 Antique Violet - med.
158	▨	828 Blue Ultra - vy. lt.
876	·	502 Blue Green
246	✕ ╱	319 Pistachio Green - vy. dk.
886	·	3047 Yellow Beige - lt.
887	∴ ╱	3046 Yellow Beige - med.
373	▼ ╱	3045 Yellow Beige - dk.
387	+	822 Beige Gray - lt.
830	○ ╱	644 Beige Gray - med.
903	✕ ╱	640 Beige Gray - vy. dk.
382	● ╱	3371 Black Brown
398	△	415 Pearl Gray
400	■	414 Steel Gray - dk.
		Step Two: Filet Cross-stitch (one strand)
301	+ ╱	744 Yellow - pale
387	○ ╱	822 Beige Gray - lt.
		Step Three: Back Stitch (one strand)
246	⌐	319 Pistachio Green - vy. dk. (two strands) (trees)
246	⌐	319 Pistachio Green - vy. dk. (name, date)
382	⌐	3371 Black Brown (all else)
		Step Four: French Knots (one strand)
246	●	319 Pistachio Green - vy. dk. (initials)
382	○	3371 Black Brown (all else)

To personalize graph, refer to alphabet on page 162.

Sisters share their inner souls,
secrets, hopes, sorrows, goals.

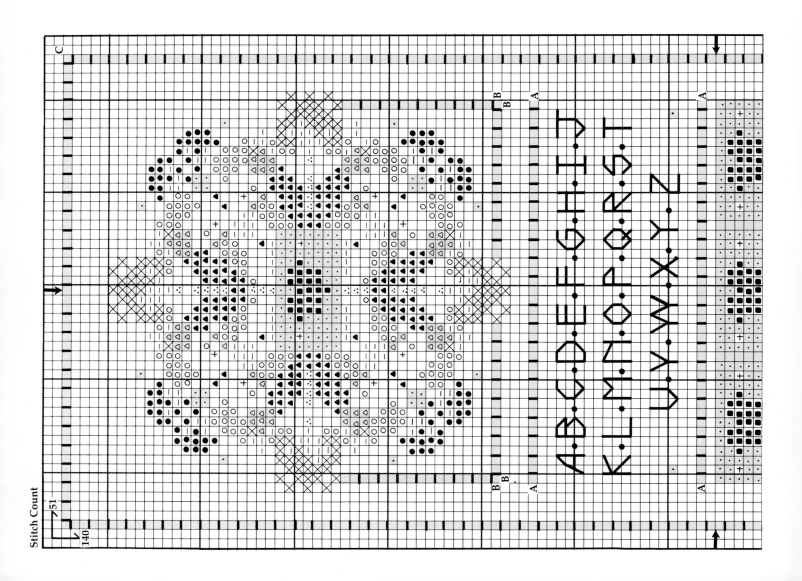

Stitch Count

51

140

FOR A SISTER

Cover Sample: Stitched on Yellow Linda 27 over two threads. Finished design size is 3¾" × 10½". Cut fabric 10" × 17". Finished design sizes using other fabrics are: Aida 11 – 4⅝" × 12¾"; Aida 14 – 3⅝" × 10"; Aida 18 – 2⅞" × 7¾"; Hardanger 22 – 2⅜" × 6¼".

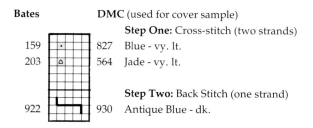

Bates		DMC (used for cover sample)	
		Step One: Cross-stitch (two strands)	
159	·	827	Blue - vy. lt.
203	△	564	Jade - vy. lt.
		Step Two: Back Stitch (one strand)	
922	⌐	930	Antique Blue - dk.

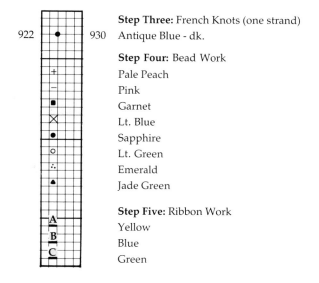

922	●	930

Step Three: French Knots (one strand)
Antique Blue - dk.

Step Four: Bead Work
Pale Peach
Pink
Garnet
Lt. Blue
Sapphire
Lt. Green
Emerald
Jade Green

Step Five: Ribbon Work
Yellow
Blue
Green

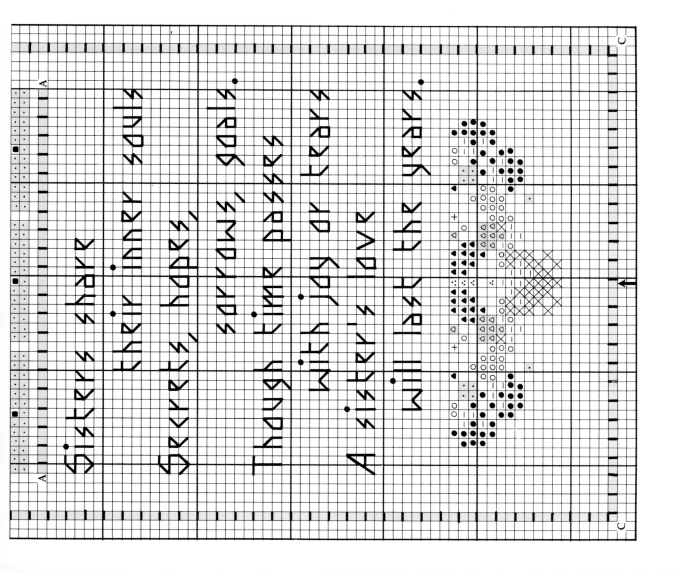

Blessed are those who can give without remembering and take without forgetting.

—Elizabeth Bibesco—

Stitch Count

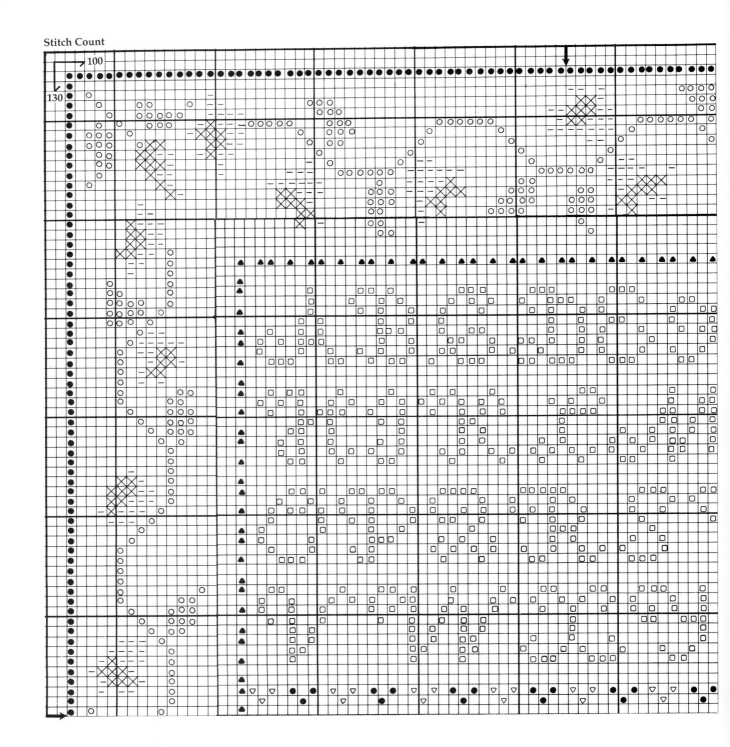

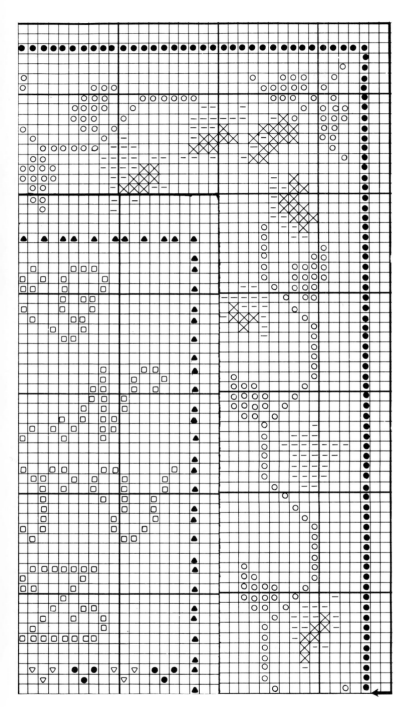

 REMEMBER ME

Cover Sample: Stitched on Black Hardanger 22 over two threads. Finished design size is 9⅛″ × 11⅞″. Cut fabric 16″ × 18″. Finished design sizes using other fabrics are: Aida 11 – 9⅛″ × 11⅞″; Aida 14 – 7⅛″ × 9¼″; Aida 18 – 5½″ × 7¼″; Hardanger 22 – 4½″ × 5⅞″.

Bates		DMC (used for cover sample)
		Step One: Cross-stitch (three strands)
66	□	3688 Mauve - med.
128	—	800 Delft - pale
130	✕	799 Delft - med.
167	▽	519 Sky Blue
168	●	518 Wedgewood - lt.
216	○	320 Pistachio Green - med.
942	▲	738 Tan - vy. lt.
		Step Two: Back Stitch (one strand)
215		368 Pistachio Green - lt. (alphabet)
66		3688 Mauve - med. (all else)
		Step Three: French Knots (one strand)
66	●	3688 Mauve - med.

To personalize graph, refer to alphabet on page 163.

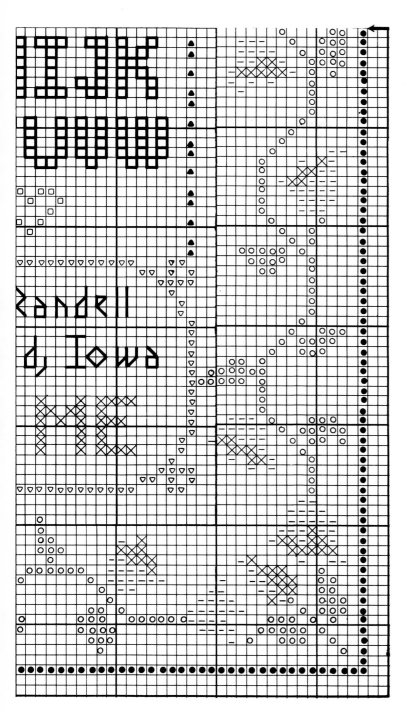

REMEMBER ME

Cover Sample: Stitched on Black Hardanger 22 over two threads. Finished design size is 9⅛" × 11⅞". Cut fabric 16" × 18". Finished design sizes using other fabrics are: Aida 11 – 9⅛" × 11⅞"; Aida 14 – 7⅛" × 9¼"; Aida 18 – 5½" × 7¼"; Hardanger 22 – 4½" × 5⅞".

Bates		DMC (used for cover sample)	
		Step One: Cross-stitch (three strands)	
66	◻	3688	Mauve - med.
128	−	800	Delft - pale
130	✕	799	Delft - med.
167	▽	519	Sky Blue
168	●	518	Wedgewood - lt.
216	○	320	Pistachio Green - med.
942	▲	738	Tan - vy. lt.
		Step Two: Back Stitch (one strand)	
215		368	Pistachio Green - lt. (alphabet)
66		3688	Mauve - med. (all else)
		Step Three: French Knots (one strand)	
66	●	3688	Mauve - med.

To personalize graph, refer to alphabet on page 163.

Faith is the substance of things hoped for,
The evidence of things not seen.

—Hebrews 11:1——

Stitch Count

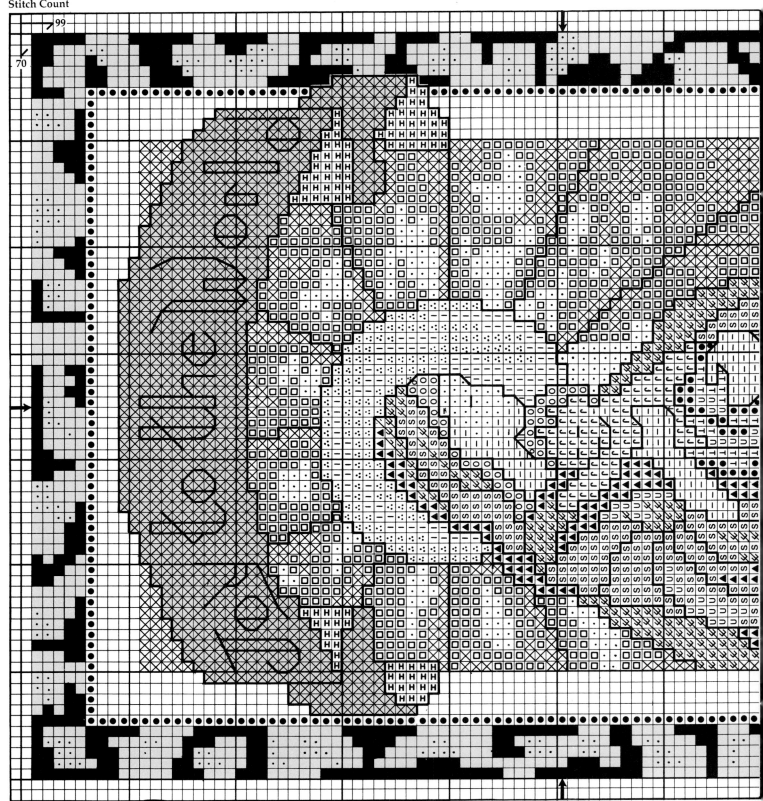

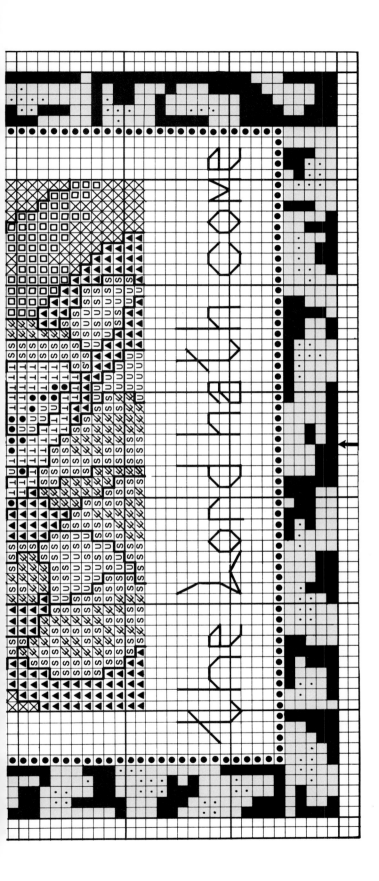

JOY TO THE WORLD

Cover Sample: Stitched on White Perforated Paper 15. Finished design size is 4⅝″ × 6⅝″. Use one 9″ × 12″ sheet perforated paper. Finished design sizes using other fabrics are: Aida 11 – 6⅜″ × 9″; Aida 14 – 5″ × 7⅛″; Aida 18 – 3⅞″ × 5½″; Hardanger 22 – 3⅛″ × 4½″.

Bates		DMC (used for cover sample)	
		Step One: Cross-stitch (three strands)	
386		746	Off White
300		745	Yellow - lt. pale
297		743	Yellow - med.
387			Ecru
366		739	Tan - ultra vy. lt.
367		738	Tan - vy. lt.
894		3354	Dusty Rose - lt.
69		3687	Mauve
70		3685	Mauve - dk.
42		309	Rose - deep
44		816	Garnet
47		321	Christmas Red
158		775	Baby Blue - lt.
149		311	Navy Blue - med.
160		813	Blue - lt.
120		794	Cornflower Blue - lt.
137		798	Delft - dk.
397		762	Pearl Gray - vy. lt.
339		920	Copper - med.
		Step Two: Back Stitch (one strand)	
403		310	Black

Merry Christmas

Lisa • Lori • Shawn

NOËL

Cover Sample on Hardanger: Stitched on Light Blue Hardanger 22 over two threads. Finished design size is 5½″ × 10⅞″. Cut fabric 12″ × 17″. Finished design sizes using other fabrics are: Aida 11 – 5½″ × 10⅞″; Aida 14 – 4⅜″ × 8½″; Aida 18 – 3⅜″ × 6⅝″; Hardanger 22 – 2¾″ × 5⅜″.

Cover Sample on Canvas: Stitched on White Needlepoint Canvas 18 over two threads. Finished design size is 6¾″ × 13½″. Cut fabric 15″ × 22″.*

Bates		DMC (used for cover sample)
		Step One: Cross-stitch (three strands)
1		White
892	225	Shell Pink - vy. lt.
40	956	Geranium
59	600	Cranberry - vy. dk.
86	3608	Plum - vy. lt.
118	340	Blue Violet - med.
119	333	Blue Violet - dk.
203	564	Jade - vy. lt.
210	562	Jade - med.
189	991	Aquamarine - dk.
362	437	Tan - lt.
936	632	Negro Flesh
		White Metallic (two strands)
		Gold Metallic (one strand)
		Step Two: Back Stitch (one strand)
59	600	Cranberry - vy. dk. (Merry Christmas)
119	333	Blue Violet - dk. (names, ground line)
203	564	Jade - vy. lt. (stems on flowers)
189	991	Aquamarine - dk. (stems in dress)
936	632	Negro Flesh (hair)
401	844	Beaver Gray - ultra dk. (people)
		White Metallic (two strands) (snowflakes)*
		Step Three: French Knots (one strand)
59	600	Cranberry - vy. dk.
119	333	Blue Violet - dk.
936	632	Negro Flesh
		Step Four: Bead Work
		Garnet
		Step Five: Couching
		Gold Metallic (garland)

*In cover sample stitched on canvas, snowflakes are stitched with two strands White Metallic and one strand DMC 800 Delft - pale (Bates 128).

NOËL

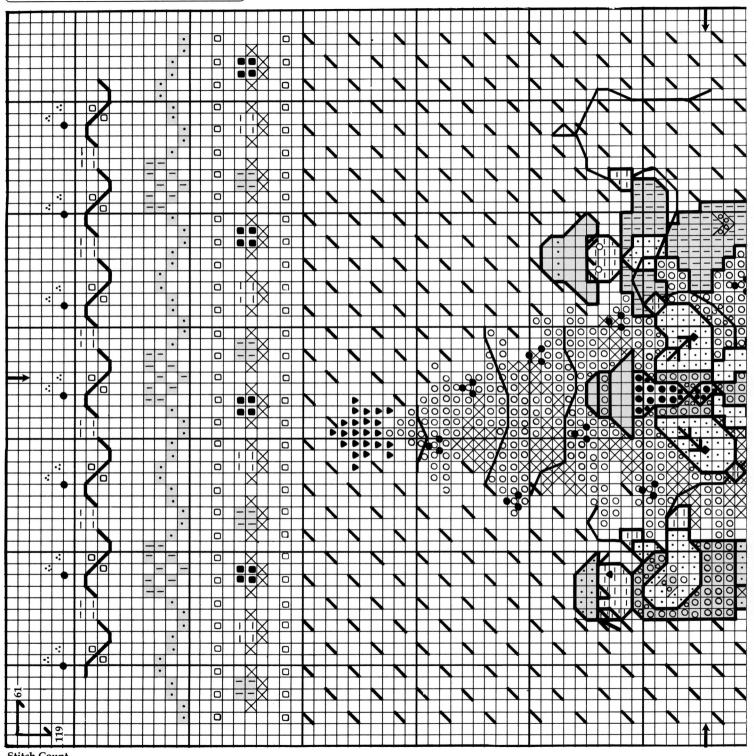

Stitch Count

To personalize graph, refer to alphabet on page 163.

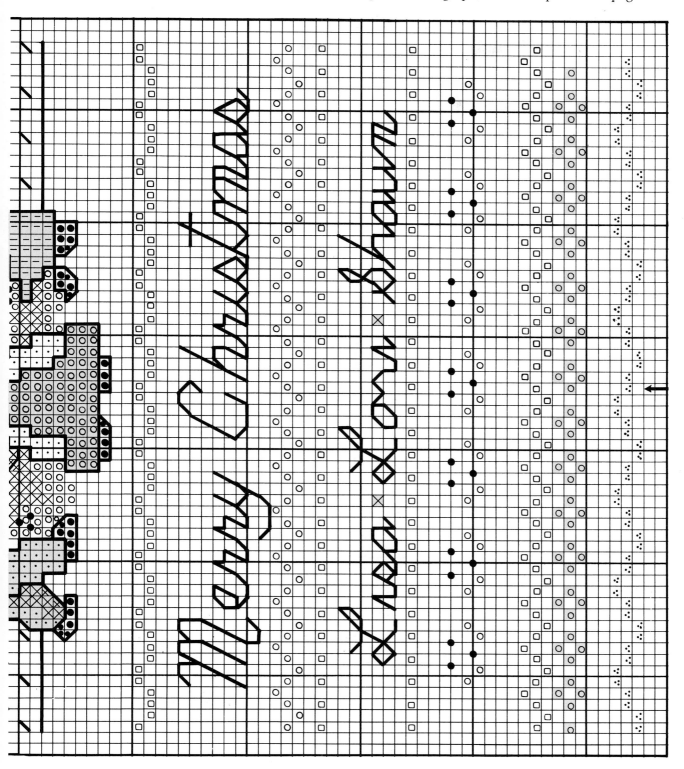

Evening hush on
Christmas dream,
Peasants seek the
gentle King.

Stitch Count

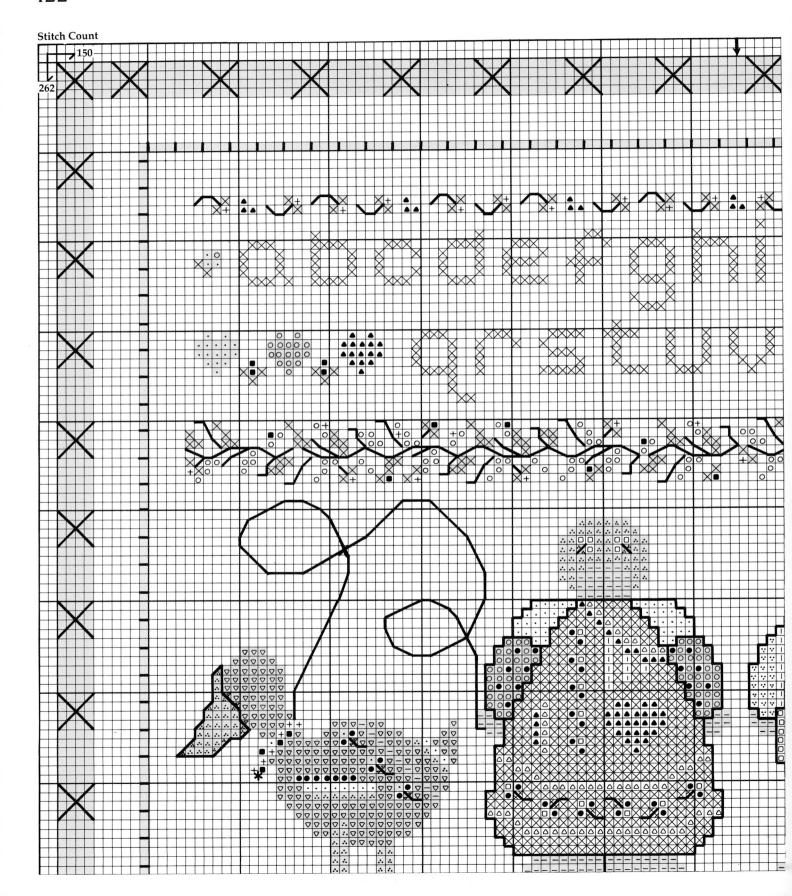

Evening hus

Christr

Peasants see

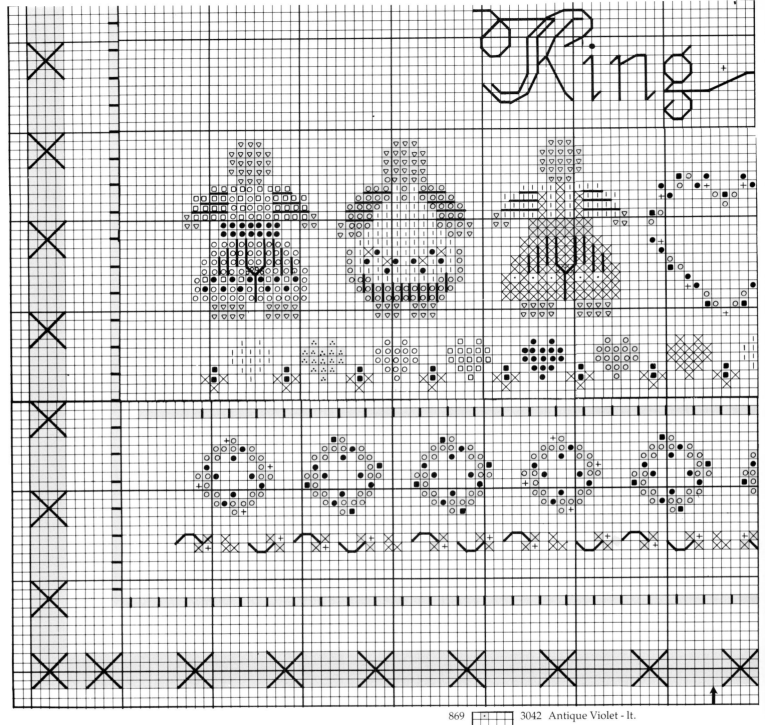

Cover Sample: Stitched on Cream Belfast Linen 32 over two threads. Finished design size is 9⅜″ × 16⅜″. Cut fabric 16″ × 23″. Finished design sizes using other fabrics are: Aida 11 – 13⅝″ × 23⅞″; Aida 14 – 10¾″ × 18¾″; Aida 18 – 8⅜″ × 14½″; Hardanger 22 – 6⅞″ × 11⅞″.

Bates		DMC (used for cover sample)	
		Step One: Cross-stitch (two strands)	
968	I	778	Antique Mauve - lt.
969	□	316	Antique Mauve - med.
970	X	315	Antique Mauve - dk.

869	·	3042	Antique Violet - lt.
920	·	932	Antique Blue - lt.
921	∴	931	Antique Blue - med.
922	∴	930	Antique Blue - dk.
150	▲	823	Navy Blue - dk.
858	○	524	Fern Green - vy. lt.
862	X	520	Fern Green - dk.
875	◐	503	Blue Green - med.
878	●	501	Blue Green - dk.
889	–	610	Drab Brown - vy. dk.
8581	▽	3023	Brown Gray - lt.
8581	△	3022	Brown Gray - med.
382	▢	3021	Brown Gray - dk.

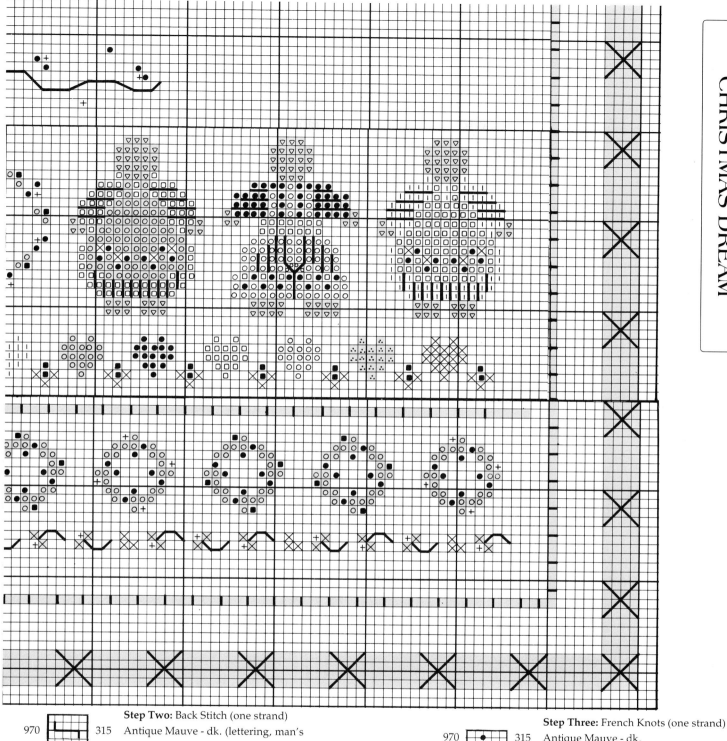

CHRISTMAS DREAM

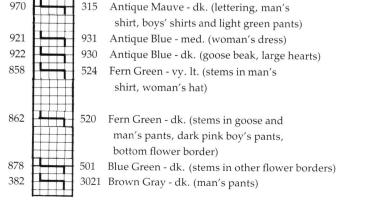

970		315	**Step Two:** Back Stitch (one strand)

Step Two: Back Stitch (one strand)

970	315	Antique Mauve - dk. (lettering, man's shirt, boys' shirts and light green pants)
921	931	Antique Blue - med. (woman's dress)
922	930	Antique Blue - dk. (goose beak, large hearts)
858	524	Fern Green - vy. lt. (stems in man's shirt, woman's hat)
862	520	Fern Green - dk. (stems in goose and man's pants, dark pink boy's pants, bottom flower border)
878	501	Blue Green - dk. (stems in other flower borders)
382	3021	Brown Gray - dk. (man's pants)

Step Three: French Knots (one strand)

970	●	315	Antique Mauve - dk.

Step Four: Bead Work

+	Coral
■	Garnet
✳	Heart (goose neck)

Step Five: Ribbon Work

Burgundy 1/16", couched with DMC 902
  Garnet - vy. dk. (one strand)
Hunter Green ¼", couched with DMC
  503 Blue Green - med. (one strand)

Step Six: Couching

Pearl Cotton #8 902 Garnet - vy. dk. (leashes)

Babies are bits of stardust...

Curtis Jonathan Shields
January 12, 1900
8 lbs. 3 ozs.

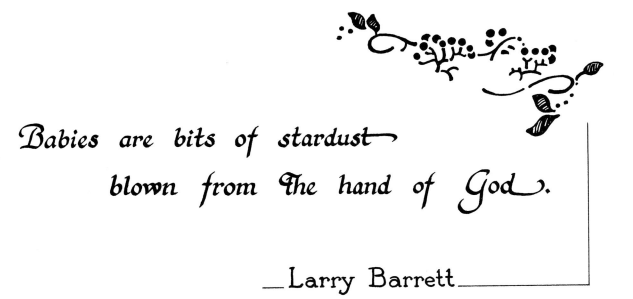

Babies are bits of stardust blown from the hand of God.

Larry Barrett

FRIENDS FOR BABY

Cover Sample: Stitched on Cream Richmond 18. Finished design size is 5¾″ × 4⅞″. Cut fabric 12″ × 11″. Finished design sizes using other fabrics are: Aida 11 – 9½″ × 8″; Aida 14 – 7⅜″ × 6¼″; Aida 18 – 5¾″ × 4⅞″; Hardanger 22 – 4¾″ × 4″.

To personalize graph, refer to alphabet on page 162.

Bates		DMC (used for cover sample)	
		Step One: Cross-stitch (two strands)	
300	·	745	Yellow - lt. pale
303	+	742	Tangerine - lt.
347	o	945	Sportsman Flesh
48	I	818	Baby Pink
24	△	776	Pink - med.
74	○	3354	Dusty Rose - lt.
42	∴	3350	Dusty Rose - vy. dk.
894		223	Shell Pink - med.
897	□	221	Shell Pink - dk.
970	●	315	Antique Mauve - dk.
871	·	3041	Antique Violet - med.
104	✕	210	Lavender - med.
101	▲	327	Antique Violet - dk.

Bates		DMC	
158	∷	828	Blue Ultra - vy. lt.
159	□	827	Blue - vy. lt.
920	−	932	Antique Blue - lt.
145	✕	334	Baby Blue - med.
876	●	502	Blue Green
914	+	3064	Sportsman Flesh - med.
		Step Two: Back Stitch (one strand)	
894		223	Shell Pink - med. (center duck)
897		221	Shell Pink - dk. (other ducks)
920		932	Antique Blue - lt. (all else)
		Step Three: French Knots (one strand)	
894	○	223	Shell Pink - med. (center duck)
897	◆	221	Shell Pink - dk. (other ducks)
920	●	932	Antique Blue - lt. (lettering)
		Step Four: Bead Work	
	▽		Pink

To me, every hour of the day and night is an unspeakably perfect miracle.

—Walt Whitman—

Stitch Count

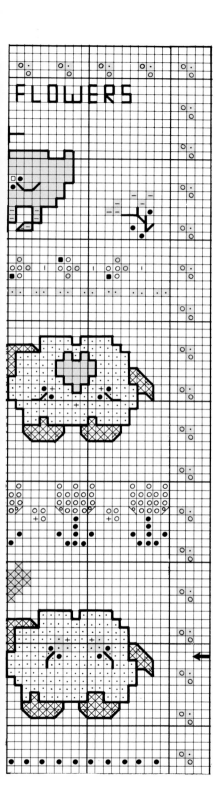

FOR AN INFANT

Cover Sample: Stitched on White Belfast Linen 32 over two threads. Finished design size is 6¾″ × 9″. Cut fabric 13″ × 15″. Finished design sizes using other fabrics are: Aida 11 – 9⅞″ × 13⅜″; Aida 14 – 7¾″ × 10½″; Aida 18 – 6″ × 8⅛″; Hardanger 22 – 4⅞″ × 6⅝″.

Bates		DMC (used for cover sample)
		Step One: Cross-stitch (two strands)
881		945 Sportsman Flesh
968		778 Antique Mauve - lt.
969		316 Antique Mauve - med.
969		316 Antique Mauve - med. (bead over cross-stitch)
970		315 Antique Mauve - dk. (bead over cross-stitch)
44		814 Garnet - dk.
869		3042 Antique Violet - lt.
920		932 Antique Blue - lt.
920		932 Antique Blue - lt. (bead over cross-stitch)
859		3053 Gray Green
846		3051 Gray Green - dk.
887		3046 Yellow Beige - med.
887		3046 Yellow Beige - med. (bead over cross-stitch)
398		415 Pearl Gray
400		414 Steel Gray - dk.
		Step Two: Back Stitch (one strand)
970		315 Antique Mauve - dk. (lettering)
920		932 Antique Blue - lt. (ribbons around geese necks)
846		3051 Gray Green - dk. (name, date, flower stems)
400		414 Steel Gray - dk. (all else)
		Step Three: French Knots (one strand)
846		3051 Gray Green - dk. (lettering)
400		414 Steel Gray - dk. (rabbit's eyes)
		Step Four: Bead Work (sewn over cross-stitch)
		Pale Peach
		Rose
		Garnet
		Light Blue

To personalize graph, refer to alphabet on page 161.

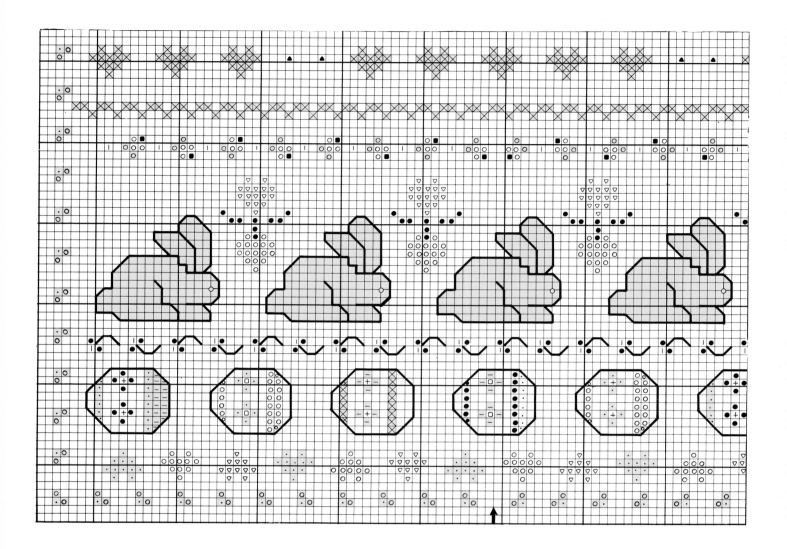

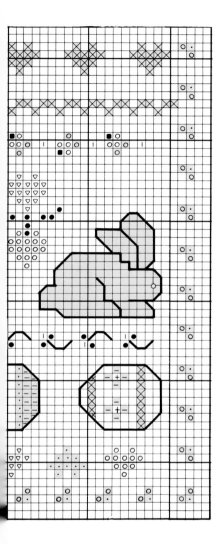

FOR AN INFANT

Cover Sample: Stitched on White Belfast Linen 32 over two threads. Finished design size is 6¾″ × 9″. Cut fabric 13″ × 15″. Finished design sizes using other fabrics are: Aida 11 – 9⅞″ × 13⅜″; Aida 14 – 7¾″ × 10½″; Aida 18 – 6″ × 8⅛″; Hardanger 22 – 4⅞″ × 6⅝″.

Bates		DMC	(used for cover sample)
		Step One:	Cross-stitch (two strands)
881		945	Sportsman Flesh
968		778	Antique Mauve - lt.
969		316	Antique Mauve - med.
969		316	Antique Mauve - med. (bead over cross-stitch)
970		315	Antique Mauve - dk. (bead over cross-stitch)
44		814	Garnet - dk.
869		3042	Antique Violet - lt.
920		932	Antique Blue - lt.
920		932	Antique Blue - lt. (bead over cross-stitch)
859		3053	Gray Green
846		3051	Gray Green - dk.
887		3046	Yellow Beige - med.
887		3046	Yellow Beige - med. (bead over cross-stitch)
398		415	Pearl Gray
400		414	Steel Gray - dk.
		Step Two:	Back Stitch (one strand)
970		315	Antique Mauve - dk. (lettering)
920		932	Antique Blue - lt. (ribbons around geese necks)
846		3051	Gray Green - dk. (name, date, flower stems)
400		414	Steel Gray - dk. (all else)
		Step Three:	French Knots (one strand)
846		3051	Gray Green - dk. (lettering)
400		414	Steel Gray - dk. (rabbit's eyes)
		Step Four:	Bead Work (sewn over cross-stitch)
			Pale Peach
			Rose
			Garnet
			Light Blue

To personalize graph, refer to alphabet on page 161.

'I love Thee'
'tis all That I can say:
It is my vision in The night,
My dreaming in The day.

—Thomas Hood——————

ABCDEFGHIJ

Sara and Justin

KLMNOPQ
RSTUVW
XYZ

A WEDDING FESTIVAL

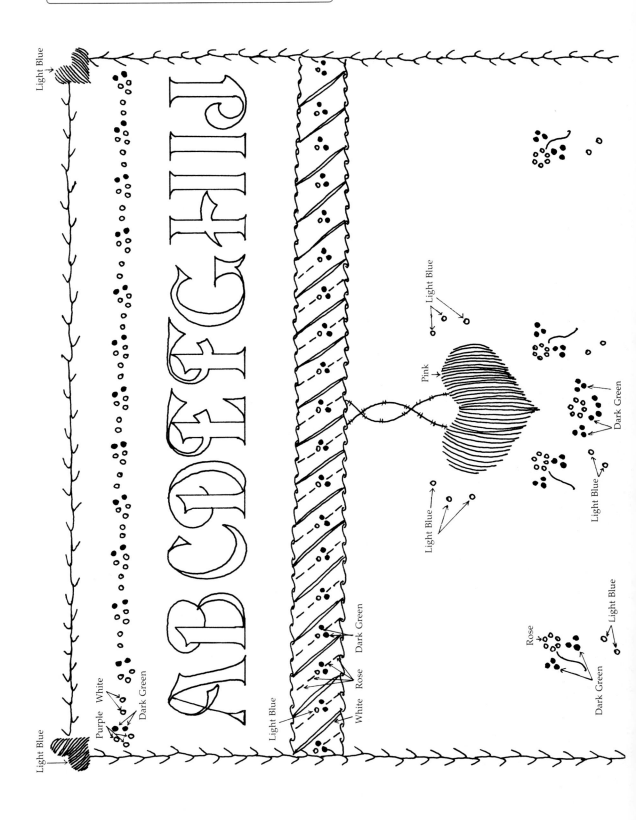

To personalize pattern, refer to alphabet on page 160.

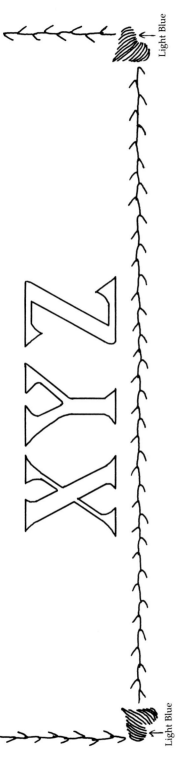

A WEDDING FESTIVAL

Cover Sample: Stitched on unbleached muslin. Finished design is 7½″ × 21½″. Cut fabric 15″ × 30″. One strand of candlewicking thread is used, except as noted. French knots are one wrap and are indicated on pattern as circles. See General Instructions for Candlewicking on page 166.

Candlewicking thread used:

White	Rose	Purple
Tan	Light Blue	Sage Green
Pink	Slate Blue	Dark Green

Man: Head, hands, and feet are Satin Stitch, using TAN. Row of hearts on shirt is Satin Stitch, using PINK thread. For row of French Knots below pink hearts, use PURPLE.

Outline of shirt is three strands ROSE thread, couched with PINK thread. Shirt sleeve is two strands LIGHT BLUE, couched with ROSE. Bands on sleeve are two strands SLATE BLUE, couched with PINK. Band across shirt is two strands PURPLE, couched with PURPLE.

Outline of pants is two strands PURPLE, couched with PURPLE. Bands on pants above flowers are two strands SLATE BLUE, couched with PINK. Band on pants below flowers is two strands ROSE, couched with ROSE.

Staff is two strands SLATE BLUE, couched with PINK. Scarves are three lines of Outline Stitch, using one strand, with colors identified on pattern.

Woman: Head, hands and feet are Satin Stitch, using TAN. Row of hearts on dress is Satin Stitch, using PINK thread. For row of French Knots below pink hearts, use PURPLE.

Outline of dress is three strands SLATE BLUE thread, couched with SLATE BLUE thread. Sleeve is three strands LIGHT BLUE, couched with SAGE GREEN. Upper and lower bands on sleeve are two strands PINK, couched with SAGE GREEN. Center band on sleeve is twisted chain stitch, using two strands SAGE GREEN.

Pocket on dress is two strands ROSE, couched with ROSE. Band across dress is two strands PURPLE, couched with PURPLE. Collar is Straight Stitch, using ROSE.

Outline of hat is Outline Stitch, using two strands PURPLE. Flower stems on hat are Outline Stitch, using DARK GREEN. Heartstrings are Twisted Chain Stitch, using one strand SLATE BLUE.

All else:

Alphabet is Satin Stitch, worked into Outline stitch on narrow lines of letters, using LIGHT BLUE thread. Names are Outline Stitch, using ROSE thread. Transfer alphabet for names from pattern on page 160.

Border is Feather Stitch, using SAGE GREEN. All hearts and tulips are Satin Stitch; colors are identified on pattern.

Horizontal borders below top alphabet row and above bottom alphabet rows are Twisted Chain Stitch, using one strand PINK. Border alternates Straight Stitch, using two strands WHITE, with Running Stitch, using ROSE.

Strings on large heart above man and woman are two strands ROSE, couched with SAGE GREEN. Stems on flowers below large heart are Back Stitch, using DARK GREEN. Stems on wreaths are DARK GREEN, couched at corners with DARK GREEN.

144

The only thing we
ever have is what
we give away.

—Louis Ginsberg—

The Oldberg's

1951

Stitch Count

129

90

STITCH NAME HERE

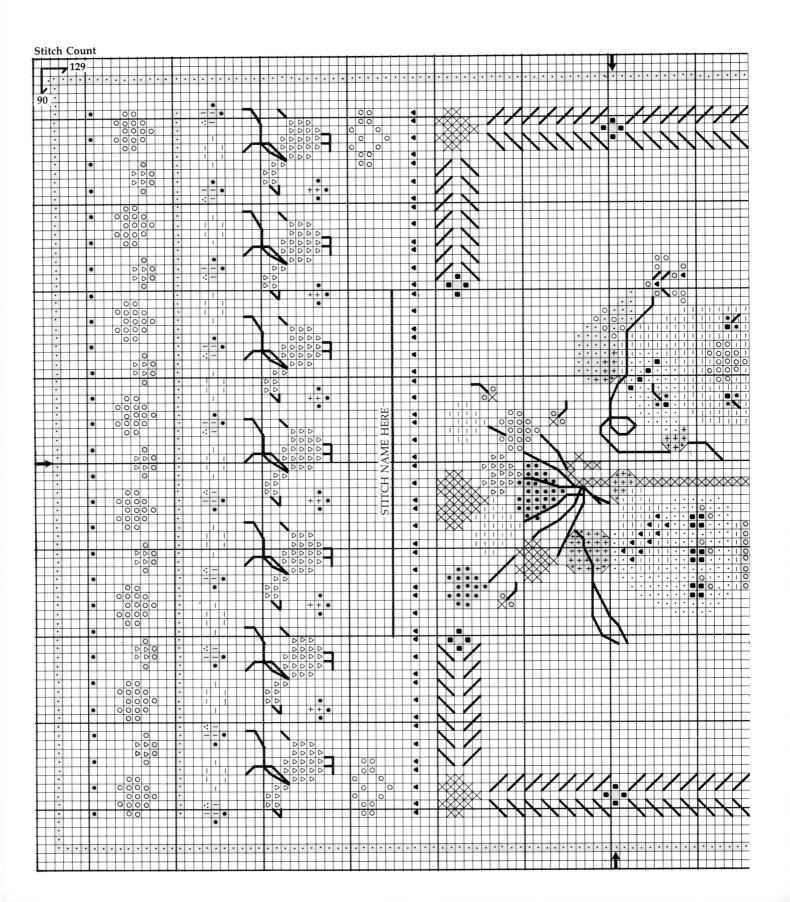

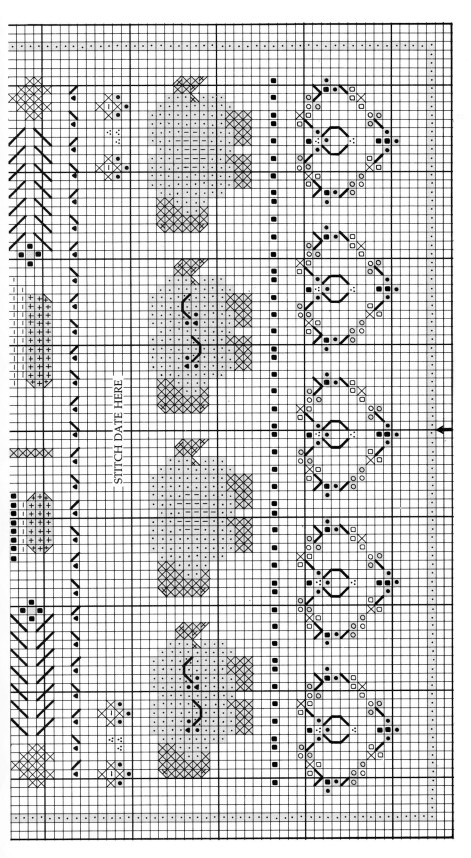

STITCH DATE HERE

A WEDDING SAMPLER

Cover Sample: Stitched on White Belfast Linen 32 over two threads. Finished design size is 5⅝″ × 8⅛″. Cut fabric 12″ × 14″. Finished design sizes using other fabrics are: Aida 11 – 8⅛″ × 11¾″; Aida 14 – 6⅜″ × 9¼″; Aida 18 – 5″ × 7⅛″; Hardanger 22 – 4¼″ × 5⅞″.

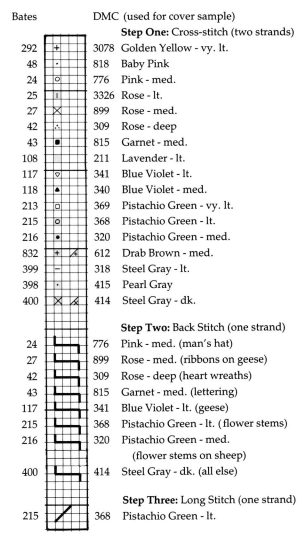

Bates		DMC	(used for cover sample)
			Step One: Cross-stitch (two strands)
292	+	3078	Golden Yellow - vy. lt.
48	·	818	Baby Pink
24	o	776	Pink - med.
25	I	3326	Rose - lt.
27	X	899	Rose - med.
42	∴	309	Rose - deep
43	■	815	Garnet - med.
108		211	Lavender - lt.
117	▽	341	Blue Violet - lt.
118	▲	340	Blue Violet - med.
213	□	369	Pistachio Green - vy. lt.
215	o	368	Pistachio Green - lt.
216	•	320	Pistachio Green - med.
832	+ ⁄	612	Drab Brown - med.
399	−	318	Steel Gray - lt.
398	·	415	Pearl Gray
400	X ⁄	414	Steel Gray - dk.
			Step Two: Back Stitch (one strand)
24		776	Pink - med. (man's hat)
27		899	Rose - med. (ribbons on geese)
42		309	Rose - deep (heart wreaths)
43		815	Garnet - med. (lettering)
117		341	Blue Violet - lt. (geese)
215		368	Pistachio Green - lt. (flower stems)
216		320	Pistachio Green - med. (flower stems on sheep)
400		414	Steel Gray - dk. (all else)
			Step Three: Long Stitch (one strand)
215	/	368	Pistachio Green - lt.

To personalize graph, refer to alphabet on page 161.

I reckon everybody wants to leave somethin' behind That'll last after They're dead and gone. It don't look like it's worthwhile to live unless you can do That.

—Aunt Jane of Kentucky—

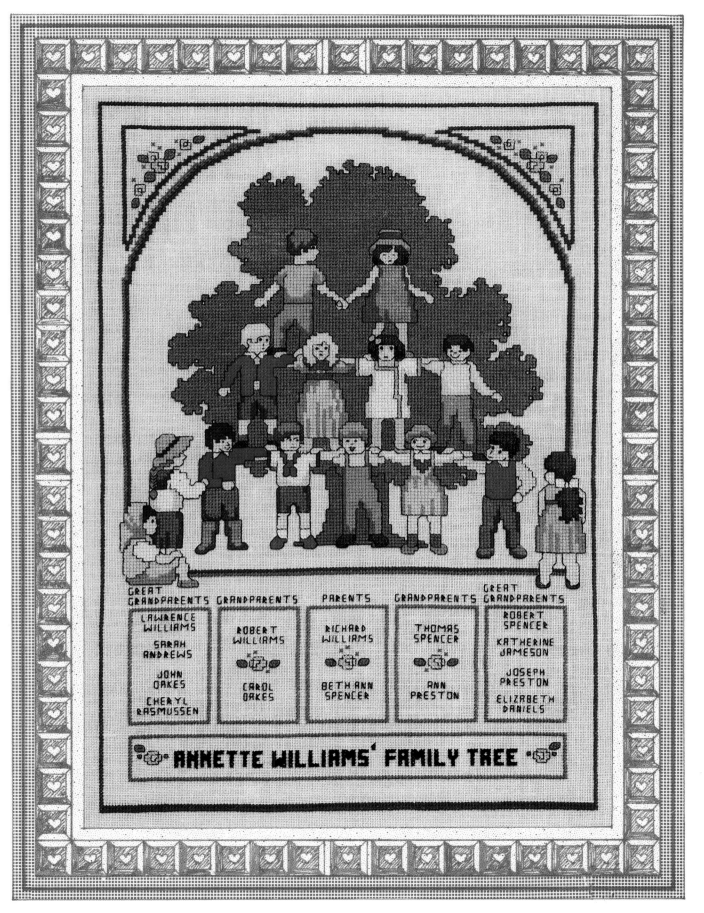

GREAT
GRANDPARENTS   GRANDPARENTS   PARENTS   GRANDPARENTS   GREAT
                                                                     GRANDPARENTS

LAWRENCE   ROBERT
WILLIAMS   SPENCER
              ROBERT   RICHARD   THOMAS
SARAH   WILLIAMS   WILLIAMS   SPENCER   KATHERINE
ANDREWS   JAMESON

JOHN   JOSEPH
OAKES   PRESTON
              CAROL   BETH ANN   ANN
CHERYL   OAKES   SPENCER   PRESTON   ELIZABETH
RASMUSSEN   DANIELS

ANNETTE WILLIAMS' FAMILY TREE

THE FAMILY TREE

Stitch Count

THE FAMILY TREE

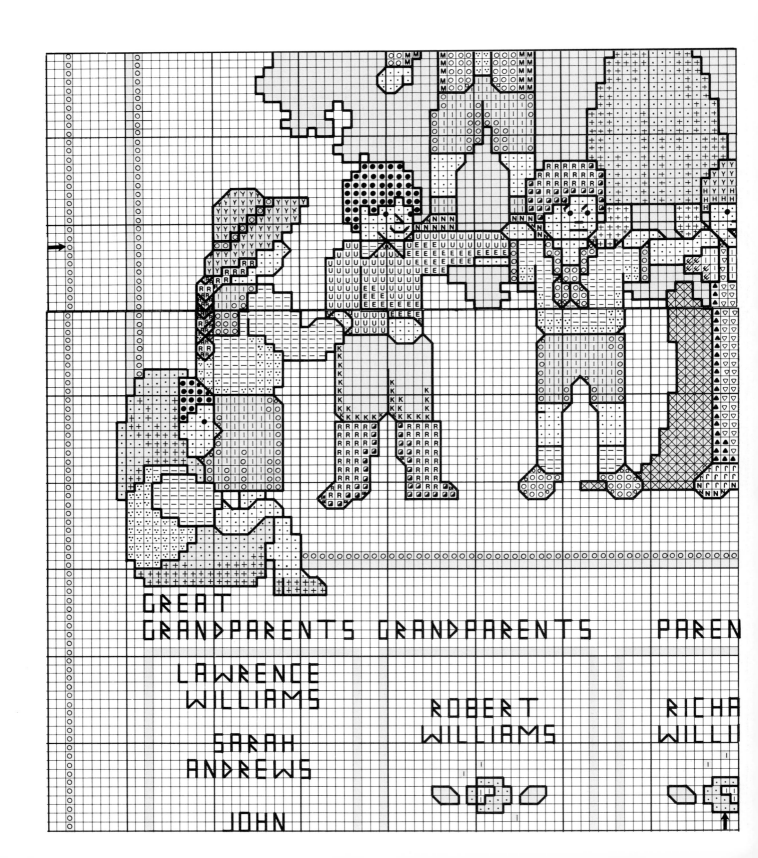

GREAT
GRANDPARENTS GRANDPARENTS   PAREN

LAWRENCE
WILLIAMS

ROBERT   RICHA
WILLIAMS   WILLI

SARAH
ANDREWS

JOHN

THE FAMILY TREE

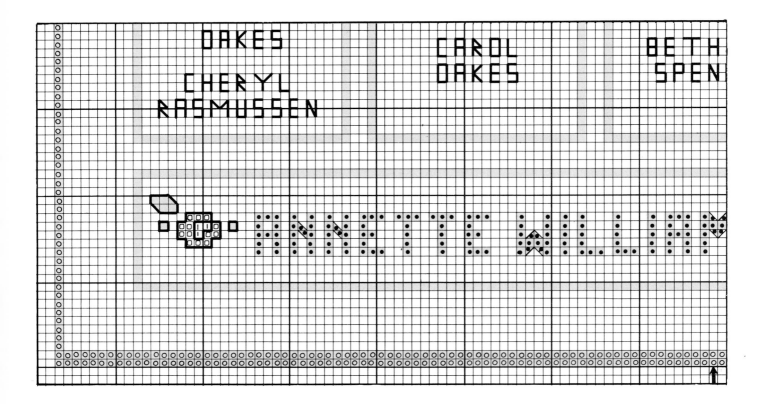

Cover Sample: Stitched on White Linen 32 over two threads. Finished design size is 9½″ × 13½″. Cut fabric 16″ × 20″. Finished design sizes using other fabrics are: Aida 11 – 13⅝″ × 19⅝″; Aida 14 – 10¾″ × 15¾″; Aida 18 – 8⅜″ × 12″; Hardanger 22 – 6¾″ × 9¾″.

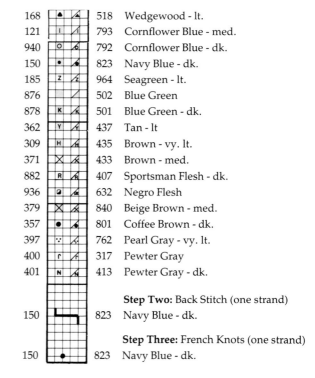

Bates			DMC (used for cover sample)
			Step One: Cross-stitch (two strands)
1	–		White
300	I		745 Yellow - lt. pale
297			743 Yellow - med.
778	·		948 Peach Flesh - vy. lt.
778	+		754 Peach Flesh - lt.
8	□		353 Peach Flesh
10	■		352 Coral - lt.
11	o		350 Coral - med.
13	M		349 Coral - dk.
47	U		321 Christmas Red
47	E		304 Christmas Red - med.
49	·		3689 Mauve - lt.
66	+		3688 Mauve - med.
95	△		554 Violet - lt.
98	∴		553 Violet - med.
158	S		747 Sky Blue - vy. lt.
167	▽		519 Sky Blue

			DMC
168	▲		518 Wedgewood - lt.
121	I		793 Cornflower Blue - med.
940	o		792 Cornflower Blue - dk.
150	·		823 Navy Blue - dk.
185	Z		964 Seagreen - lt.
876			502 Blue Green
878	K		501 Blue Green - dk.
362	Y		437 Tan - lt.
309	H		435 Brown - vy. lt.
371	X		433 Brown - med.
882	R		407 Sportsman Flesh - dk.
936	▣		632 Negro Flesh
379	X		840 Beige Brown - med.
357	●		801 Coffee Brown - dk.
397	∴		762 Pearl Gray - vy. lt.
400	Γ		317 Pewter Gray
401	N		413 Pewter Gray - dk.
			Step Two: Back Stitch (one strand)
150	⌐		823 Navy Blue - dk.
			Step Three: French Knots (one strand)
150	●		823 Navy Blue - dk.

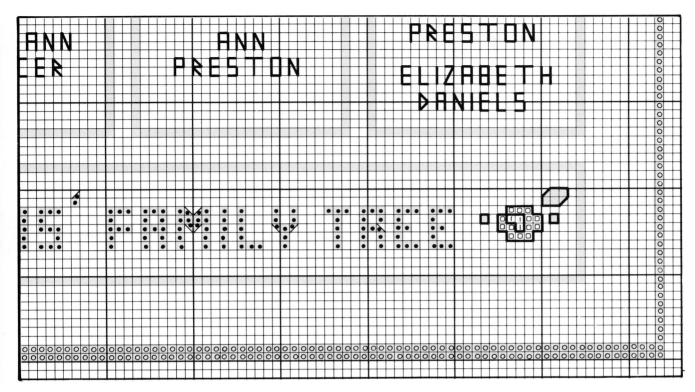

To stitch an initial or name, transfer letters to graph
paper. Mark centers of graph and begin stitching in
center of space indicated for personalizing.

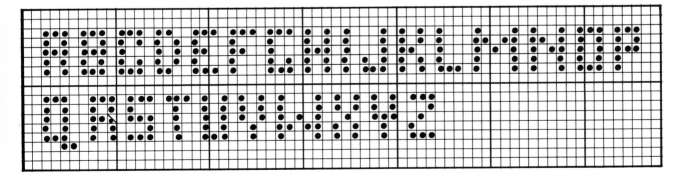

Where is the heart that doth not keep
Within its inmost core;
Some fond remembrance hidden deep
Of days that are no more.

—Ellen C. Howarth—

a b c d e f g h i j k

The Bass Family

107

149

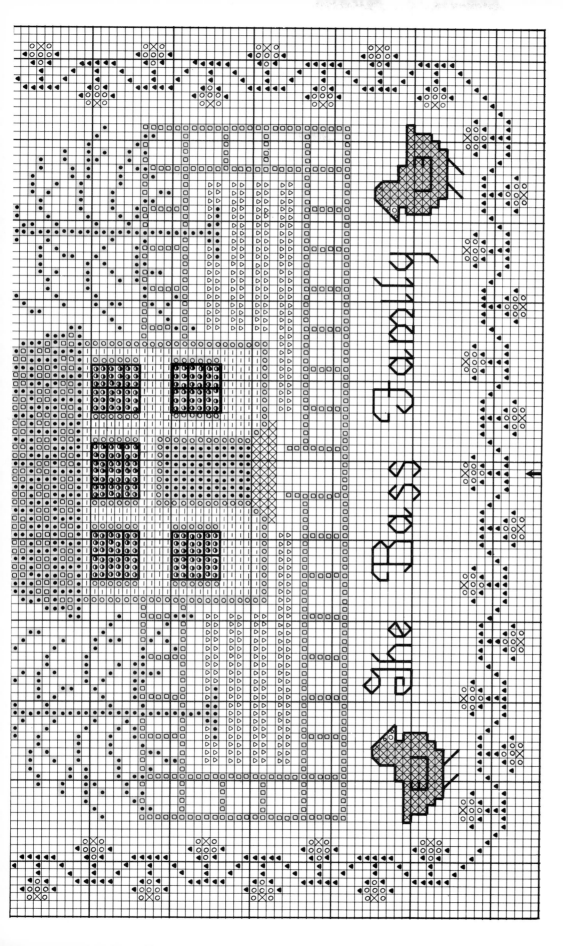

To adjust design to represent a specific family, stitch parents in center as they appear on graph and add children on either side, using graphed children as patterns.

To personalize graph, refer to alphabet on page 162.

OUR FAMILY TRADITION

ALPHABETS

Cover Sample: Stitched on Light Brown Linen 26 over two threads. Finished design size is 8¼" × 11⅜". Cut fabric 15" × 18". Finished design sizes using other fabrics are: Aida 11 – 9¾" × 13⅝"; Aida 14 – 7⅝" × 10⅝"; Aida 18 – 6" × 8¼"; Hardanger 22 – 4⅞" × 6¾".

To cross-stitch an initial or name, transfer letters to graph paper. Mark centers of graph and begin stitching in center of space indicated for personalizing.

Bates			DMC	(used for cover sample)
			Step One: Cross-stitch (two strands)	
387			712	Cream
366			951	Sportsman Flesh - vy. lt.
886			677	Old Gold - vy. lt.
893			224	Shell Pink - lt.
894			223	Shell Pink - med.
970			315	Antique Mauve - dk.
921			931	Antique Blue - med.
875			503	Blue Green - med.
876			502	Blue Green
363			436	Tan
830			644	Beige Gray - med.
392			642	Beige Gray - dk.
889			610	Drab Brown - vy. dk.
			Step Two: Back Stitch (one strand)	
970			315	Antique Mauve - dk. (girl's apron, baskets)
889			610	Drab Brown - vy. dk. (all else)

For use with A WEDDING FESTIVAL, page 140.

a b c d e f g h
i j k l m n o p q
r s t u v w x y z
1 2 3 4 5 6
and 7 8 9 0

A B C D E F G H I J
K L M N O P Q R
S T U V W X Y Z

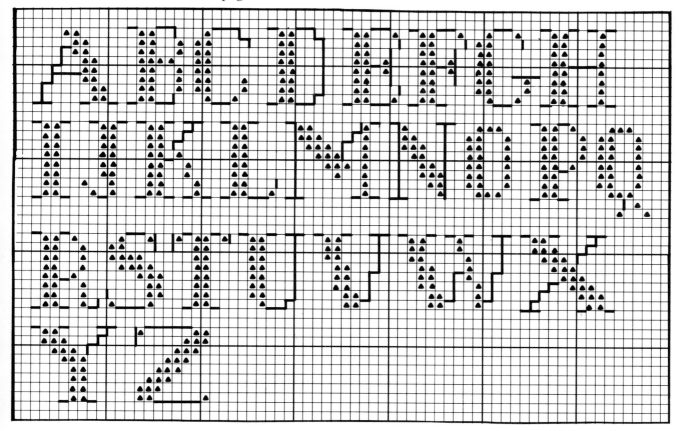

For use with FOR AN INFANT, page 134, and A WEDDING SAMPLER, page 146.

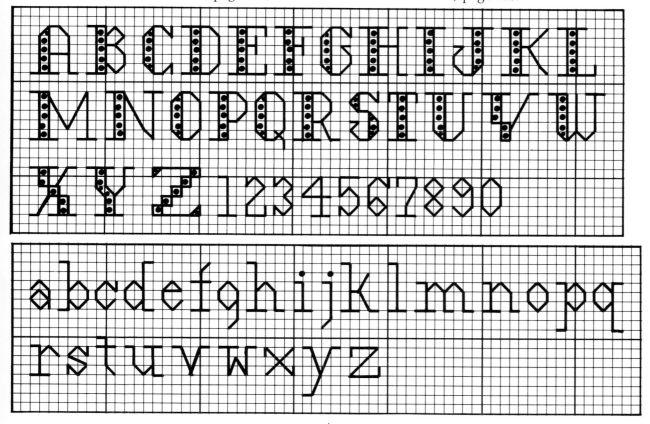

ALPHABETS

For use with FRIENDS FOR BABY, page 130, and OUR FAMILY TRADITION, page 158.

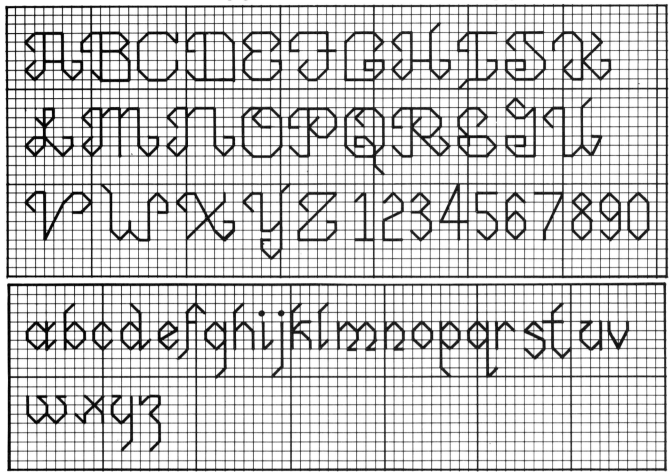

Numbers to use in dating graphs as desired.

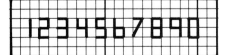

For use with A SAMPLER FOR A FRIEND, page 34.

For use with THE BIG HORN SHEEP, page 98, and A SAMPLER FOR A FRIEND, page 34.

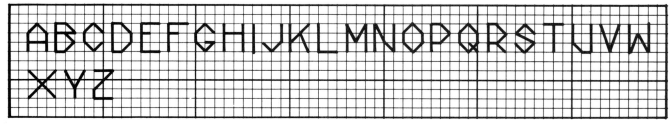

For use with NOËL, page 118.

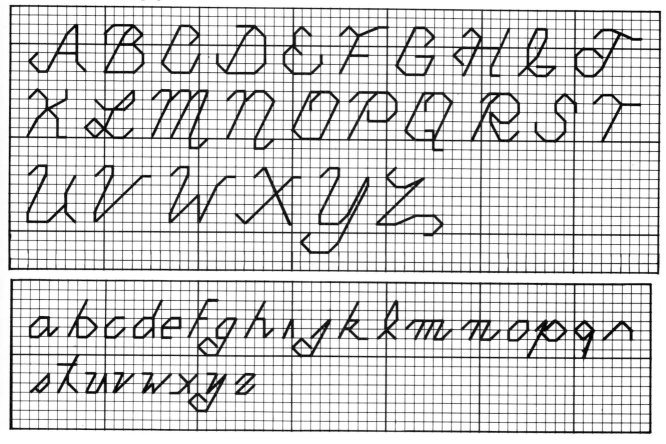

For use with FROM THE PAST, page 18, and REMEMBER ME, page 108.

For use with REMEMBER ME, page 108.

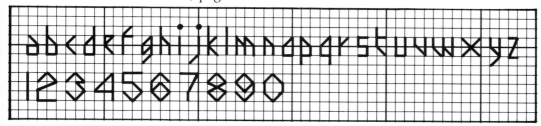

For use with FROM THE PAST, page 18.

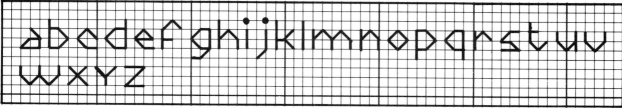

GENERAL INSTRUCTIONS

CROSS-STITCH

FABRICS: Most fabrics used in this book are evenweave fabrics made especially for cross-stitch and are available in needlework departments or shops. Fabrics used in the models in the photographs are identified in the cover sample information by color, name and thread count per inch.

NEEDLES: Use a blunt tapestry needle which slips easily through holes in fabric and does not pierce fabric. With fabric having eleven or fewer threads per inch, use needle size 24 or 26; with eighteen threads or more per inch, use needle size 26.

PREPARING FABRIC: Cut fabric 3″ larger on all sides than design size or cut as indicated in cover sample information. To keep fabric from fraying, whip stitch or machine zigzag raw edges.

HOOP OR FRAME: Select frame or stretcher bars large enough to hold entire design. Place screw or clamp or hoop in 10 o'clock position (or 2 o'clock, if left handed) to keep from catching.

FLOSS: Cut floss into 18″ lengths. For best coverage, run floss over damp sponge and separate all six strands of floss. Put back together number of strands recommended for use in cover sample information. Floss will cover best when lying flat. If twisted, drop needle and allow floss to unwind.

CENTERING DESIGN: Find center of fabric by folding from top to bottom and again from left to right. Place pin in point of fold to mark center. Locate center of graph by following vertical and horizontal arrows. Begin stitching at center point of graph and fabric. Each square on graph represents one complete cross-stitch. Unless indicated otherwise in cover sample information, each stitch is over one unit of thread.

SECURING FLOSS: Never knot floss unless working on clothing. Hold 1″ of thread behind fabric and secure with first few stitches. To secure end of thread, run under four or more stitches on back of design.

READING GRAPHS: To help distinguish colors in designs, shade graphs with colored pencils.

BACK STITCHING: Complete all cross-stitches before working back stitches or accent stitches. When back stitching, use number of strands indicated in code or one strand fewer than used for cross-stitch.

STITCHING METHOD: Use "push and pull" method for smoothest stitch. Push needle straight down and completely through fabric before pulling up.

CARRYING FLOSS: Do not carry floss more than ½″ between stitched areas. Loose threads, especially dark ones, will show through fabric. When carrying floss, run under worked stitches on back side when possible.

CLEANING COMPLETED WORK: After making sure fabric and floss are colorfast, briefly soak completed work in cold water. If soiled, wash gently in mild soap. Roll work in towel to remove excess water; do not wring. Place work face down on dry, lightweight towel and, with iron on warm setting, press until work is dry.

STEP 1: Cross-Stitch — Bring needle and thread up at A, down at B, up at C, and down again at D; see Diagram 1. For rows of cross-stitch, stitch across entire row so floss is angled from lower left to upper right, then return; see Diagram 2. ALL STITCHES MUST LIE IN THE SAME DIRECTION.

Diagram 1   Diagram 2

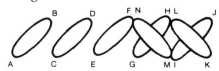

Half-Cross — Indicated on graph by slanted line with color symbol beside it (see Diagram 1), make longer stitch in direction of slanted line.

Diagram 1

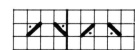

The stitch actually fits three-fourths of the area; see Diagram 2. Bring needle and thread up at A, down at B, up at C, and down at D.

Diagram 2

In cases where two colors meet, the graph will be similar to Diagram 3. The stitched area will look like Diagram 4.

Diagram 3   Diagram 4

STEP 2: Back Stitch — Working from left to right with one strand of floss (unless designated otherwise in code), bring needle and thread up at A, down at B, and up again at C. Going back down at A, continue in this manner; see Diagram 1.

Diagram 1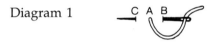

STEP 3: French Knot

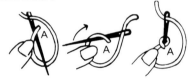

STEP 4: Bead Work — Attach beads to fabric with a half-cross, lower left to upper right. Secure beads by returning thread through beads, lower right to upper left. Complete row of half-crosses before returning to secure all beads.

FILET CROSS-STITCH

FILET CROSS-STITCH is a modern interpretation of a lacemaking technique called "filet brode." When complete, the background resembles a delicate net. The design is cross-stitched with enough strands of embroidery floss to cover the fabric while the background is ordinarily stitched with one strand. Designs having a definite positive and negative pattern work best.

LAID RIBBON WORK

Complete stitching as shown on graph. Where laid ribbon is indicated, pin ribbon over length of fabric and complete stitching over ribbon; see Diagram 1. Trim excess ribbon. For cross-stitch pieces, cross-stitch over ribbon.

Diagram 1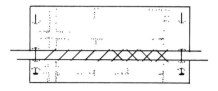

CHICKEN-SCRATCH

CHICKEN-SCRATCH is traditionally worked on woven gingham fabric, which is available in fabric stores. Gingham fabric is patterned in three values: light, medium and dark. Although the gingham pattern may appear to be in squares, the pattern actually is made up of rectangles. Therefore, when cutting gingham according to measurements in cover sample information, cut with vertical edges of design parallel to selvage or position fabric to cut with number of rectangles fewer to the vertical inch than to the horizontal inch.

NEEDLES: Use a size 26 tapestry needle.

STITCHING: Find center of fabric by folding from top to bottom and again from side to side. Find starting point, indicated by "C," in center of graph. Note color of fabric square to be covered by first stitch by referring to Step 1 of code. This will situate your stitching over the correct color of fabric. Continue stitching following steps of code. Refer to code for color of floss, number of strands and stitch to be worked. Keep tension of stitches fairly loose so as not to pucker fabric.

Woven-Stitch — Indicated on graph by four straight lines with symbol in center designating color; see Diagram 1.

Diagram 1

Straight lines stand for straight stitching. Complete straight stitches first; see Diagram 2.

Diagram 2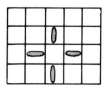

Bring needle up at A, weave needle underneath each straight stitch to form a circle, take needle down at A; see Diagram 3.

Diagram 3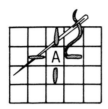

To avoid puckering, do not pull circle too tightly. Completed stitch will look like Diagram 4.

Diagram 4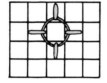

Smyrna-Cross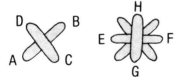

Partial Smyrna-Cross

FILET CROCHET

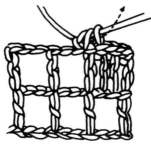

Filet Crochet

Abbreviations
ch — chain stitch
dc — double crochet
sk — skip

CANDLEWICKING

CANDLEWICKING, labeled as truly American needlework, was born of necessity. When embroidery yarns and canvases became scarce in nineteenth-century America, women used the soft cotton yard they had on hand for candlemaking to embellish their homes. Most often, candlewicking was undyed yarn on matching fabric. However, plants were sometimes used to produce a wide range of soft colors. Once stitched, the work was washed and the shrinkage secured the embroidery.

FABRICS: Candlewicking is stitched on unwashed, 100% cotton muslin. Muslin is manufactured in natural and a variety of muted colors. Cut fabric larger than needed to allow for shrinkage. See cover sample information for sizes of fabrics used in models.

NEEDLES: Use a crewel embroidery needle.

PATTERNS: Patterns in this book are full-size. Center fabric over pattern and, keeping fabric smooth, trace with water-soluble dressmaker's pen. Dressmaker's chalk may be used on dark fabrics.

THREAD: Candlewicking thread is 100% cotton and manufactured in four-strand units. Available colors vary between brands. Use the number of strands indicated in individual codes.

STITCHING: Center fabric in hoop large enough to encompass entire design. Stitch from center out following code for specific stitches.

SHRINKING: Shrinking fabric is essential to candlewicking and adds dimension to the finished work. Rinse design piece in cold water to remove pen lines. Then rinse in hot water. While still wet, place RIGHT side down on thick towel. Place press cloth over WRONG side and iron with moderate iron until dry.

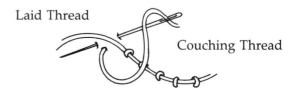

Laid Thread

Couching Thread

Laid Thread / Couching

Twisted Chain

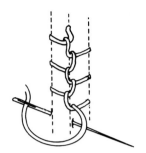

Feather Stitch

Straight Stitch

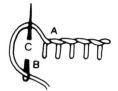

Blanket Stitch

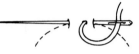

Backstitch

Satin Stitch

Lazy Daisy Stitch

Outline Stitch

French Knot

All fabrics available to shop owners from
  Joan Toggitt
  35 Fairfield Place
  West Caldwell, NJ 07006

Perforated paper available to shop owners from
  Astor Place
  239 Main Avenue
  Stirling, NJ 07980

Beads available to shop owners from
  MPR Associates
  P.O. Box 7343
  High Point, NC 27264

Ribbon available to shop owners from
  C.M. Offray & Son
  Route 24, Box 601
  Chester, NJ 07930-0601

INDEX